"I love the way Ron looks at himself, and thus the world, through refreshingly honest self-talk, and then dialogues with me, the reader, with a full amount of caffeinated energy. The book is evidence that humor, honesty, and introspection have all the makings for a great read—a great read that helps us to be more authentic as we engage in our own extended journey on the java trail of life."

—RON KUEST, soul-mentor, coach, and coauthor of *Gravity: Seven Essential Truths About Influence, Leadership, and Your Soul*

"Brace yourself for a fresh perspective on faith—an upgrade on the ways we Christians interact with the world. Biblical? Check. Humble? Check. Global? Refreshingly so. Like an ordained barista, DeMiglio serves nothing but the steaming hot truth with a dollop of dry wit and some freshly baked tales. Are you ready to engage with Jesus in all the places coffee grows or gets sold? Grab a mug. The first sips may be slightly disorienting but you'll line up for refills, I promise you."

—LORI STANLEY ROELEVELD, blogger, coffee-lover, and author of *Jesus and the Beanstalk*, *Running from a Crazy Man*, and *Red Pen Redemption*

"Buckle your seat belt and prepare to see the world with Ron DeMiglio. Meet people, taste the coffee, and be ready for the last sip that causes you to shun common thinking. Each chapter is a tour stop in a new city in this travel adventure of discovery, where Ron's humor is a spoonful of sugar to help the wisdom go down."

—MARTY FOLSOM, executive director of the Pacific Association for Theological Studies

"To say DeMiglio stirs an oversize pot and chuckles while he does it is an understatement. At the same time, his challenging, inspiring, sobering, sometimes irritating (because he strikes so close to home), and laugh-out-loud stories will—without question—change your life in profound ways. Highly recommended."

—JAMES L. RUBART, best-selling author of *The Five Times I Met Myself*

COFFEE
THE
World
and
JESUS

BUT NOT NECESSARILY IN THAT ORDER

Ron DeMiglio

Kregel
Publications

ISBN 978-0-8254-4465-4

Printed in the United States of America
17 18 19 20 21 22 23 24 25 26 / 5 4 3 2 1

This book is dedicated to my wife, Tina.
After all these years, after all our adventures, after raising
children, after making money and going broke, after all the
laughs, tears, missteps, and victories, I still get butterflies when I
hold your hand. You make me feel capable.

Contents

Introduction
A-Parrot-ly, It's Not About Me

For the past twenty-five years, my life, in one way or another, has been about coffee—buying, selling, roasting, serving, and loving coffee. Most of those years were spent working in the international coffee industry. Coffee has taken me quite literally all over the world. I not only love the taste and smell of coffee (roasted coffee, that is; green coffee smells like wet hay) but I also love the business of coffee, I love the people of coffee.

This is not, however, a book about coffee. It's a book about a Jesus-following peddler of that golden arabica elixir and how other worldviews, peoples, and cultures transformed my faith—one cup, one country, and one person at a time.

A Cagey Tactic

If all this makes me sound like some kind of a world-wise exotic traveler, talk to my friends and family. They'll set the record straight.

I'm just a guy. A guy who has been blessed with the privilege of making a living in the coffee industry while traveling the world.

I didn't always have this balanced of a perspective. In the beginning of my career, I thought I was a pretty big wheel of cheese. I covered up my walk of pride by deflecting compliments and feigning embarrassment at accolades. But inside I sucked them in like a black hole.

Maddeningly it seemed like every time I opted to relax, revel, and bask in the glow of the creature-length film that was my life, Jesus started kicking the back of my seat. *Thump!* "You are mine." *Thump!* "I love you." *Thump!* "Hear my call." *Thump!* "I've got much more for you." *Thump!* "That soda will weaken your bone density." (The last one might have been my wife prayerfully tilling the me-dirt. But the other kicks were definitely Jesus.) Ha!

That man is truly relentless.

I recall an event that, for me, highlighted just how persistent Jesus has been in my life. It was on my second trip to Japan that I was scheduled to meet with a prestigious trading company in downtown Tokyo. I sported a new suit and an old attitude. I had my international businessman savvy ratcheted up to industrial strength and I was a force to be reckoned with, or so I thought. Smug and cocky, I was not the least bit prepared for Jesus to interject himself again.

I had memorized a few social graces in Japanese on my flight over the Pacific. I was really going to wow these guys. They wouldn't know what hit them. As I stepped off the elevator, a receptionist confirmed my appointment and invited me to sit in one of their lavish lobby chairs. Aside from the receptionist, I was the only one in the waiting area. Only the fortunate few got to sit in these chairs. Me. How big cheesy was I now!

As I waited, my eyes scanned the area. In the corner was a large, ornate birdcage that held a stunningly beautiful parrot. The parrot looked as regal and formidable as I felt at that moment. Motionless, the bird stared at me. Its colors were so vibrant, it almost didn't look real. It all felt so international and exclusive. I was in my element.

Then it happened.

Without warning the parrot rattled off three full sentences of flawless Japanese. Holy blazing beak, Batman! The parrot knew more Japanese than I did and its pronunciation was perfect.

My preening, puffy persona evaporated instantly. I sat there trying to reclaim my business swag but it was too late. God had effectively used a lobby parrot to snap me back to the knowledge that this wasn't about me at all. Never was about me. In an instant, I decreased (deflated really) so that God might increase. His void-filling assurance and peace were instantaneous.

To say I didn't see that coming would be an understatement. I was so used to Jesus's surprisingly pointy sandals in the small of my back that this event caught me totally off guard. Sometimes you just have to give it up to God—especially when he takes you by complete surprise. I smiled inside and tipped my metaphoric cap.

humbled

That incident was one of my wake-up calls. For the first time in a while, it startled me so much, I didn't hit the snooze button. There were a few more incidents that I'll cover in this book, but that event was the first serious step in my heart change.

Some people have asked if I feel silly for thinking that the God who created the universe took the time to concern himself with my attitude before my business meeting.

No. No, I do not.

He's God. It's what he's capable of and what he said he would do for me. He promised he would give me the desires of my heart. I believe he was just getting my heart right first so my desires could be right. I count on him holding me accountable at all times. It's unnerving, but by proclaiming Jesus as Lord and Savior, I've given him that latitude in my life.

At that moment, God was just being God.

A Hill of Beans

Over the years, God has used the most unexpected means of fostering perspective and humility in me and, with them, greater effectiveness for his kingdom. I want to share a little of what I've learned in some of the most lavish and destitute places on earth. Allow me to tell you how I've been shamed by the richest people I've met and inspired by the poorest—and vice versa. And all the while, I've been figuring out this whole Jesus, grace, mercy, love, and gospel thing.

I have grown in the places where coffee grows. I have flourished and failed in the rich social soil of the coffee-buying and -consuming regions of the world. And I don't feel the least bit out-there when it comes to acknowledging the means God has employed in keeping me on point.

Nothing about the God I serve is predictable or common. Spotting my Savior's hand in the obscure and trivial makes me feel uncommonly loved. So much so that I developed a two-word phrase that keeps me alert to the subtlety of God in my life. The phrase is "Shun Common." It keeps me mindful of his attentive, uncommon presence, so I've decided to end every chapter with the phrase. It's more for me than for you. But if you want to make it your own, no worries here, my friend. Isn't sharing fun?

Okay, I'm ready. Let's do this book thingy.

Join me on my coffee journey. Allow me to tell you what I learned and how my travels gave me the peripheral vision to get acquainted with a bigger Jesus than my American upbringing allowed—a Jesus that created coffee and loves the people of coffee even more than I do.

Shun Common

Chapter: A Distant Chili Dog

Location: Yokohama, Japan

Purpose: Scouting Coffee Shop Locations

Getting lost on foot in Yokohama, Japan, was disturbing.

I'd checked into my hotel and made my way to my room on the twenty-third floor. The view was spectacular and the sheer density of the region drew me in like jumbo shrimp at a wedding reception. As I scanned the city I spied the top half of a baseball stadium that looked closer than it really was. It had to be the home of the Yokohama BayStars. I didn't have anything to do for several hours so I put on comfy foot treads and hit the mean streets of Yokohama. Finding the stadium was simple, as the lobby staff pointed me in the general direction.

I walked around the entire baseball complex several times and took in the atmosphere of the historic baseball stadium. But after circling it I wasn't completely sure which street I had taken to get there. The streets all looked the same—narrow and jammed with buildings, people, and businesses.

The buildings were so tall and the streets so narrow that I couldn't get my bearings or see anything beyond my immediate location.

Blazing Trails and Annoying Strangers

Was I worried? Nah. Not me. I was Lewis and Clark! My Japanese was reasonable enough to figure out the path back.

Or so I thought.

This was different. I wasn't in a meeting with businesspeople who spoke some English. I was on the streets of Yokohama, not just out of my comfort zone but out of my comfort continent.

People on the street responded to my questions about getting back

13

to my hotel with a few quick hand gestures and verbal instructions that approached spin-cycle speed. It was exasperating and escalated my dislike of mimes. I can't explain why. It just did. They spoke so fast they might as well have been speaking Klingon. "Lewis and Clark" had just been exposed as "Clueless and Lark." The bits and pieces I could understand meant almost nothing to me. I had no clue where the landmarks were that they referenced.

I felt completely out of my element, yet everyone around me was in the center of theirs. It took me an hour and a half and involved enough distance to make even Forrest Gump pucker, but eventually I stumbled across my hotel again.

A Turf Warrior

My circuitous adventure that day poked its head into my consciousness door a short time later—but when it happened again, I was the one with the home field advantage.

My original business partner is Japanese. Over the past twenty-five years, I've been to Japan many times to see him, and he's been to the United States frequently. But since his last trip I had moved my office, so he needed new directions.

He called me from the airport the morning he arrived. We agreed to meet in a familiar place and then he'd follow me to my new office. I rattled off all the potential meeting sites I felt certain he would know.

He didn't know any of them.

So I rattled off a few of Seattle's major landmarks along the I-5 corridor and suggested we meet near one of them.

Didn't help.

His response was the same to every suggestion . . . silence followed by, "I don't know where that is."

Just before I suggested we resort to smoke signals from a dumpster fire, I said, "Is there any place in town that you *do* know?"

He was quiet for a moment then blurted out, "Yes! Yes! Weiner-schnitzel!"

If you're not aware, Weinerschnitzel is a US chain of quick-serve hot-dog restaurants. I happened to know the store he was talking about. But to say the location was obscure would be like saying that Neptune gets a little nippy once the sun goes down. He'd only been there twice in twenty-five years. How could he remember how to get to a little hot-dog joint when he couldn't figure out how to get to a navigable body of water?

Simple. He loved their chili dogs. So it became a familiar landmark to him. It was a reference point, a part of his vocabulary, a marker he understood.

What I thought were obvious landmarks meant nothing to him. Then it hit me like a ton of bok choy. (A ton is a ton, right?) I was self-ishly enamored with my own reference points. They were the appropriate ones—the right ones—for my life, but not for my friend.

The first thing I should have asked was, "What place do you know how to get to?"

It never occurred to me to think about what might be a reference point for him and him alone. And what's easier? For him to find my landmarks, or for me—a lifelong Seattleite—to find his?

My Sunday Smooth

This whole reference-point thing feels strangely familiar. I confess, when I'm around unsaved folks, sometimes I feel like I'm in the middle of a foreign city where I don't speak the language. But at church? That's home. I've had Sundays where everything I utter to my fellow believers feels like pure gold. There's an ease to my rapport and nothing has ever felt more natural.

Then Monday rolls around. Emboldened after getting my Sunday smooth on, I decide to share Jesus with a stranger. Suddenly, every word I sputter seems as appropriate as telling a ten-year-old reading *Old Yeller* that the dog dies in the end.

A fictional conversation (but one I sometimes feel capable of): "Excuse me, sir, but are you aware that God loves you and has a wonderful plan for your life? Well . . . I'm not saying the plan you've devised for your own life is complete rubbish, but it wouldn't hurt to consider an alternative, right? Sorry. That didn't come out right. Can I start over? Have you ever thought about where you'll go after you die? Really, you were just diagnosed with pancreatic cancer? You don't say. Huh. So this is a timely topic for you? Time out. That wasn't the response I was looking for. Why are your fists clenched? Oh, shoot. How forgetful of me. I had a poppy seed muffin for breakfast and I really need to floss. Let's catch up later. Bye!"

Everything I say sounds contrived, insensitive, and way out of place. What is it about sharing my faith with non-Christians that instantly turns me into the biggest shovelhead in the shed?

Maybe, just maybe, it might be as simple as realizing that when it comes to Christianity, nonbelievers might be standing on the befuddling streets of their own Yokohama—without a landmark in sight.

Who Hid the Heathen?

Maybe that's the crux of my Monday blunder. Maybe that's why I so often feel lost in Yokohama when sharing my faith.

My point of reference is always the cross. When talking and ministering to other Christians, I naturally share the same understanding of where to head. My point of reference doesn't, or at least shouldn't, change. The ultimate destination for almost every substantive conversation, concern, or solution always ends at the foot of the cross. But when I engage the unsaved, they naturally share no such understanding or reference point.

If I want my words and actions to impact a nonbeliever, I need to consider the other person first. (Novel idea, huh?) Where are they spiritually? What do they know or not know? What do they believe or not believe? Where can I most effectively meet them in order to show the love of Christ? If I would simply ask questions and discover where their own personal landmarks are, amazing things can happen.

My words must cease to be limited to the catchphrase or fear-based arguments I've defaulted to in the past. You know the ones:

· Turn to Jesus or burn in hell—the Christian version of Stockholm syndrome

- God said it, I believe it, that settles it!—the all-purpose default balm that soothes any painful lapses in effort or logic
- Pascal's Wager—the idea, when you boil it down, that Christianity might be a waste of time, but it can't hurt!

Don't get all highbrow on me.

The Roman's Road? The four spiritual laws? Admit it! You've either used them or have at least considered using them as you picture your friends auto-falling to their knees in the wake of your brilliant verbal snippet or lovingly compelling point. I've done it all too often!

Amazingly, when I've taken the time to meet others where they are and talk about what they know, the cross is always visible. I've never needed to do anything more than engage people in normal, value-extending conversation.

It's really that simple.

I don't need to force the issue. When I've met people where they are, the conversation suddenly feels natural and easy. I've had completely ordained conversations with people that wore more leather than a cow or had more ink in their skin than an octopus. I've bantered with and befriended people so unlike myself that, at first, it made them suspicious. I've talked about life with tough guys who were bigger than my first apartment as well as the painfully shy among us.

I once struck up a conversation with a legless man in a wheelchair who was menacingly eyeing people from the entrance of an alley. As I approached him, the smell of alcohol, body odor, and urine hit me like a giant stink-hammer. I knelt beside him and asked if there was any way that I could serve him. His facial expression softened immediately as he asked me if I could reposition his pillow and help him sit more upright because his back was hurting. I did, and the cross made an appearance.

Like atomic clockwork, I can count on it.

A nonbeliever may only know where to find a chili dog. So what? Meet them there with me. To be perfectly frank, I need to love the unsaved enough to meet them in their own ballpark. (Sorry, couldn't resist a couple of hot-dog puns.) Then my words will have real substance and effect.

I don't increase my odds of being heard by dragging people onto my own reference turf. I'll never find the people who really need to hear about Christ by only frequenting my boardroom comfort zones.

Go Fetch the Rest

Jesus didn't shy away from unfamiliar streets. He sought out and ministered to the adulterous woman at the well. We don't have community wells anymore, so spend some time at the local watering hole, park, transit center, coffee shop, smoke shop, or hot-dog stand. Discover where the marginalized and forgotten hang out in your community. Go get uncomfortable for Jesus. Maybe find a bar and join a darts league, hand out ice-cold water or soda at a skate park, go play checkers with a forgotten someone at a nursing home, or dress up like a Christmas tree and stand in the middle of a public library just to thumb your nose at "the man."

Ignore that last one, please—although I've personally considered doing it.

Sure, I might periodically feel as out of place as a NASCAR sticker on a Prius as I rationally discuss the sanctity of my marriage with a lifelong gay friend. Yep, that happened. That's okay. I need to get used to it. The Bible tells me that I can be different and still emit light and fit in.

Wanna join me?

Knew you did. Cool. Let's find the chili dog in the lives of the lost and hurting. I'm pretty sure it won't ruin my church cred to Weinerschnitzel it now and then.

Shun Common

Chapter: Stop Quivering

Location: Buraydah, Saudi Arabia

Purpose: Training Employees

This is officially the most frightening trip I've ever been on.

I have four armed bodyguards watching out for me at all times. They were provided by the local government to ensure my safety. And, yes, they are absolutely necessary. I was hesitant when I agreed to this trip. Now I know why. Americans are not thought of highly here.

I feel sad about that. I'm being deprived of the things I love most. I don't get to freely interact with the locals or see any of the surrounding area. In addition to training employees, I'm being driven around the countryside to approve future coffee shop locations. But when we arrive at each spot, they won't let me get out of the car until they have formed a security perimeter.

It turns out Buraydah is a far different place than Riyadh, Saudi Arabia. In Riyadh, you see people from other countries. Not many, but you do see them. You also see women. Again, not many. The ones you do see are modestly dressed, if not in full burkas. Some Saudi men dress in Western clothes but the majority of men in Riyadh still wear traditional Saudi attire. (It looks really comfortable.)

In Buraydah the men only wear traditional Saudi attire. I wore slacks and a button-down shirt. Oh joy, it's more than just the color of my skin that makes me stick out like a nun at Mardi Gras.

There are no women to be seen. Anywhere. The city seems bereft of public estrogen.

Okay, I saw one woman during my entire stay. One. We were in a restaurant and they brought her in a side door and quickly ushered her to her table behind a black screen. Once she was seated at the table, the black screen was then used as a visual barrier. The process they used to conceal her was well orchestrated and elaborate. Women here are forbidden to drive and are never allowed to work in this part of the world. Their lives unfold, from beginning to end, behind closed doors and screens. I can't imagine the struggle they must endure.

The majority of Saudi men don't work either. They mostly sit around in parks and hotel lobbies and talk during the day. It's a nice life.

Almost all manual labor is done by imported servants from other countries, and all because they have oil in their ground. The locals refer to oil as "God's blessing." I found it to be one of the cruelest curses imaginable. Not that the laborers are slaves; everyone I saw was of legal age. Most applied to work here and seemed happy. But from the outside, it appears to be an artificial world of entitlement and leisure.

It's 124 degrees today. I think the locals must have an asbestos coating on the backs of their thighs and rear ends. The seats are so hot I can't figure out how to get in a car and not break-dance for the first sixty seconds.

Yes, inside the car. It's not attractive.

The heat soaks away my energy and makes my mind sluggish. Plus I can't walk any distance without my security detail's approval, and goat meat and dates prepared a different way for every meal is wearing on me.

I had a bit of an attitude.

The hotel where I'm staying is lavish. I can only imagine how enjoyable it would be if they would turn on the air-conditioning. Two minutes. That's all I need.

There are only two places in the hotel I'm allowed to hang out for any length of time: my room or the game room in the basement. "Game room" is a lofty term for a concrete basement with a few chairs and a Ping-Pong table. Even in the hotel my movement is restricted. What had I gotten myself into?

I was frustrated. There were people I wanted to spend time with. History and sites I wanted to experience. I understood it could be dangerous for me so I didn't press the issue. But I felt trapped.

"Get into the coffee industry," they had said. "You can see the world!"

Funny, I didn't see those people here.

Captive, Yet Again

This might shock you, but I also used to feel trapped when reading about the full armor of God in Ephesians 6:10–18.

I'm not kidding. Don't get indignant. I'll explain.

The reason I felt trapped by that section of Scripture has to do with the specific words Paul used: in verses 16–17 Paul says, "In addition to all this, take up the shield of faith, with which you can extinguish all the flaming arrows of the evil one. Take the helmet of salvation and the sword of the Spirit, which is the word of God."

Does it bother anyone else that the enemy has arrows (flaming arrows, mind you), a weapon used at a distance, while the only offensive weapon I have (the sword) requires close proximity to do any damage?

The evil one can fire arrows at me from afar but I'm stuck trying to lure him into an arm's-length confrontation. What kind of playing field is that? Far from level, it seemed. I want a godly grenade, a Holy Ghost howitzer, or an Abba Father flamethrower! Give me something, Lord! My enemy is pelting me from the shadows with flaming arrows and I'm stuck here impersonating a ceiling fan.

Was I trapped in my room and unable to move freely yet again? No. Like my time in Buraydah, I needed to find the beauty that was right in front of me. Hidden in plain sight.

Shadow Tickling

I was in a familiar place. My mind was perceiving a nuance in a section of Scripture and I needed to figure out what God wanted to teach me. I was certain there was a spiritual truth here that would fuel my frustration fire at being cooped up and guarded in this city. I just needed to identify it so I could expose the appropriate party. The way I see the world is an attribute that has paid dividends in my own walk and occasionally in the walk of those with whom I share my insight. I was sure this would be another such epiphany moment.

I was wrong about that.

I tend to recall my God moments like I do sports and card games I've played. The ones I remember most vividly involved my victory. The times when I've lost or failed all but disappear from my memory.

I'm pretty sure it's an attribute that doesn't serve me as well as I like to think it does.

Tactical Envy

This issue? The truth? The insight? Gossip.

God said to me: Let me be blindingly clear. If you gossip in any fashion, you have willingly lowered yourself to the preferred, from-a-distance battle tactics of Satan and are firing his flaming death arrows at the body of Christ. Stop attacking your fellow soldiers with something as insidious as gossip. It's not beneficial to the body of Christ and, if you engage in it, neither are you.

Ouch. Medic!

Hold the phone, Lord! I'm not a guy given to gossip. I feel on top of that one. What's this really about, Lord?

God: "Keep writing."

Okay, I Will

God: "What do you call it when you make sweeping generalizations or insensitive comments regarding other countries, people, and cultures?"

Me: "Astute observations and playful insight?"

God: "Try again, please."

Me: [deep sigh] "Attacks from afar?"

God: "Yes. Ron, I love and miss those people with whom I sent you to work. I miss them more than you could possibly imagine. They're my precious creation and my love for them knows no bounds. I am just as involved in their lives as I am yours. Distance does not give you the right to mock. Poke, prod, tease, and quip—it's all good. But do it within the confines of my Word. Words and humor can heal or they can destroy. There is no middle ground. You can say hard things, if they're marinated in my love. Find that balance."

Me: "I get it. I'll do my best. Thank you, Lord."

Adore the Sword

Ephesians 4:29 says, "Do not let any unwholesome talk come out of your mouths, but only what is helpful for building others up according to their needs, that it may benefit those who listen."

Ah, I get it, God. I think you were telling me that I wasn't trapped in Buraydah, I was just limited in the people you wanted me to touch. And my purpose there wasn't to be a tourist or scratch my adventure itch; it was to be an ambassador for you.

God: "So far, so good."

And I'm not trapped or pinned down by flaming arrows from my enemies either. You have given me a shield of faith to fend those off. So if my conversation follows the tone you asked of me in Ephesians 4:29, I don't need to worry about the enemy's arrows or shoot any myself.

God: "Keep going."

No long-distance weapons? Who cares! Security detail and restriction of movement? So what! Neither of those things kept me from operating freely in the place where I was, with Christlike love and ministering grace.

God: "He can be taught!"

God: "One More Thing, Ron"

I wasn't trapped in Buraydah and I'm not trapped by the armor of God. And I need to quit telling myself that I am. I was exactly where God wanted me to be: fighting with the exact weapons he wanted me to use.

The reality of this trip was that I was in a country with some people that many perceive as dangerous. But a curious thing happened in the midst of the sun, sand, and security detail. I grew to love and enjoy the people of Saudi Arabia. And I think that makes me the dangerous one.

Thank you, Lord, for that insight.

Shun Common

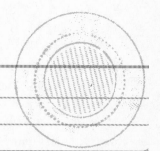

Chapter: Money Changer
Location: San José, Costa Rica
Purpose: Sourcing Coffee

Costa Rica seems slightly schizophrenic to me. Stop. I think of myself as eclectic, so don't go there. The airport felt like Florida. Most everyone spoke English, and the local currency is not the US dollar but might as well be. Most places there accept it.

Costa Rica is a Central American country with a beautiful culture and rich history. But it's also as close to a wholly owned subsidiary of the United States as a country can be and still keep its own distinct cultural identity. I wanted to like the country but there was something askew. I could feel it.

Swimming Up Currency

Why was it that I just couldn't get in sync with this place? I mean, the tropical climate is amazing! As a general rule, white sand, azure water, and brightly colored birds make me involuntarily grin. In Costa Rica, all my visual food groups were represented, so I should have felt eye-nourished.

I didn't.

Maybe it's that Costa Rica feels like an uncomfortable combination of Central and North America. Or it might be the money that bothers me about Costa Rica.

Scratch that.

It's definitely the money thing. I don't want to use US currency. I want my international currency-exchange experience. If a country has its own exclusive currency, then it has its own economy. If it has its own economy, then it's a country. I suppose it's just that silly. What's the deal with money, anyway? Why does Costa Rica seem a little less authentic to me just because of my familiarity with the dominant currency?

I think it's because American money attracts Americans, and not always your average Americans. International travel and business is by and large the playground of the affluent and privileged—and unfortunately a few of them, from time to time, can be an insufferable, snotty lot of bipeds. It embarrasses me a little.

You Ain't Got No Joy, Boy

I like being in other countries for a number of reasons, but the one that impacts me most is the level of contentedness in the poor. I've spent time with whole families who lived in a ten-by-ten-foot shack with no doors or windows, just openings, and they were content and joyful. Their joy felt real, fresh.

There are always the disgruntled outliers, but for the most part I've found the poor in poor countries are happy people. They are gruntled. They have work and enough food to exist, very little more. Yet they are not lacking in joy. It's convicted me on more than one occasion. I've been poor and happy. I've been well-off and happy. But I'm not sure I've been as content as these people.

Money's not as important to me today as it is to most Americans, but compared to the citizens of the poorer countries of the world I feel like the most self-absorbed heretic in the economic sandbox.

Dead Precedence

Why is money such a weird thing? Seriously. It warps me. It seems to warp most of us. Whether from a lack of it or an abundance of it or an intense desire to live at either extreme. We have whole church movements centered on prosperity as a sign of holiness or poverty as the only path to an authentic Christlike existence.

The love of money is the root of all kinds of evil. Why is the love of money the root of all kinds of evil?

Here's my take: people like what money appears to buy. I don't mean possessions or hangers-on—or embarrassingly old men with twentysomething wives. (Like a nice shirt, a functional marriage cannot be both wrinkled and wrinkle free. I'm just saying.)

When I say people like what money appears to buy, I mean power and influence. Isn't that what the Serpent really enticed Eve with? By eating the fruit, their eyes would be open and they could be like God. It may not have been what we classically consider money, but it was a transaction nonetheless.

Something was offered, and a price was paid. Still is.

The Company We Keep

We separate classes of people based on nothing but money. Oh, I know people with lots of money like to believe that the distinction between them and others is based on more than wealth, but it's not. Money does that to people. Some poor people like to believe that they are more honest and virtuous than the wealthy, but they're not. All the dividing lines we like to attribute to money, or the lack thereof, have little basis in reality. Stripped down and basic, or flashy and loaded with accessories, we're all still broken people.

Sir Richer of Poorer

I once heard a radio show about how the majority of young people who enlist in the military come from relatively poor upbringings. They took call after call on the subject, and the thoughts about it were as divided as the neighborhoods that people live in.

One older lady called in and angrily proclaimed she felt safer with poor people in the military because poor people were more resilient and resourceful. I thought that a strange statement. The next thing that popped into my mind was if they were so resourceful, they wouldn't be poor—which was, of course, equally bigoted. When that money train sped past me, I got sucked onto the tracks of division so fast that it shocked me. I didn't like the feeling.

Why does money make us want to choose sides? Money has no power beyond that which we ascribe to it. It's only money. Maybe it's because so much of how we see ourselves in the United States is tied to money. I don't think God sees the color green. He's a jealous God, not an envious one.

Dirty Little Secrets

In February 2010, *Forbes* magazine did a story on a workplace phenomenon called "imposter syndrome." The story focused on highly paid female executives, but the condition is not gender specific. These highly paid executives often have the belief they are fooling other people, "faking it," or getting by because they have the right contacts or are just plain lucky. Many believe they'll be exposed as frauds or fakes. Impostor syndrome goes far beyond normal bouts of self-doubt. Deep down these people knew they had worked hard but, in some capacity, believed they had stumbled into their position and wealth.

I suspect that's probably true.

But that self-doubt is not the persona these people portray. They act assured and confident. I wonder if any of us are ever completely real when money is involved. In some small or big way, money tweaks all of us.

Even worse, it feels like we can't win when it comes to a holistic, biblical view of money. Being prudent with money is clearly encouraged in Scripture. But so is giving it all away. Growing our money would provide more money to give away for a longer period of time, but that means saying no to some people. That's the part that would be the most difficult for me.

The Money Mirage

In spite of what Wall Street or *Forbes* would tell us, money doesn't really buy anyone power. That's its hook. It buys the illusion of power. Money, like political leadership, is ultimately acquired and lost at the behest of God and for his sovereign will to be accomplished. Seeing money for what it is loosens its grip on me.

I want you to do something right now. Think of the biggest power brokers in the world today. Got a few people in mind? I was serious.

Ready? Now imagine you're dead and have been for many years. You and God are chatting and he motions with his eyes toward a faraway earth. You haven't thought about earth for years (whatever those are). You can tell by his expression that he's asking what you see down there on the planet you once called home. It forces you to think about something you haven't considered for who knows how long: the fallen existence of the once majestic. Now, in this context, consider the power brokers I just asked you to think about.

Got the mental picture?

Pretty funny, huh? From that vantage point, the whole scene would be almost comical. They would look like the silliest of people, scurrying around doing the silliest of things, for the silliest of reasons, and accomplishing the silliest of results, frantically gathering kingdoms of fog. Hosting formal events to give each other awards while wearing clothes that others told them they should wear and saying hollow things that, by definition, have been stripped of anything meaningful. Power brokers? Really? More like desperate inhabitants of an elaborate ant farm.

The Broke in Broken

I have met people whose identity in Christ is inseparable from their limited economic status. So much so that they would sabotage any significant opportunity out of instinct to keep their poverty vows intact and visible. That's no less silly than the power brokers.

Is it possible to see God as a dependable and benevolent provider if we squander what we have to avoid the appearance of means? Again I ask, why is money such a weird thing?

Desiring wealth and influence for their own sake is not a Christ-centered motivation either. Seeking to honor God with the excellence of your effort and skill may well result in wealth, but you'll likely have a heart that's more capable of experiencing his pleasure and direction.

Shunning wealth and influence is no less self-serving. Fearing gain is still living in fear. But being leery or cautious when it comes to those things is wisdom.

I don't want to be like what Costa Rica has become. Costa Rica is an unusual mix of Western influence and Latin culture. It exists with one foot in both worlds. I don't want to walk the tightrope between money and authenticity, but I don't want to hold that tightrope walk against a beautiful land like Costa Rica based on what their government has done. I'll hold any money I have loosely. In reality, it was never really mine in the first place. Money's only real purpose is to bring God glory and build bridges that connect people to Jesus Christ.

The country of Costa Rica is incredibly beautiful, and its people are wonderful. The fact that something as innocuous as money tainted it for me tells me that no matter how far I've come, money still tweaks me just a little.

I'll keep working on it.

Greater Equals Lesser

Has anyone else noticed that the presidents who did the most for early America are depicted on the smallest notes? The size of the currency appears to be in inverse value to the contribution of the person on the face of it.

I just noticed that recently, and the instant I did a previously dislodged shard of understanding found its natural place in my spirit. I felt like God told me the less importance I place on money, or denominations of currency, the greater the value my contribution to his kingdom will end up being. With that last statement in mind, I'll let you noodle on the double meaning of the word *denomination*.

Forgive me, Costa Rica. Money still claws little rifts in my psyche. I shouldn't have held your currency against you. This one's on me. And I hear you have your own pretty pictured money and everything! Way to go, CR!

············ *Shun Common* ···

Chapter: The Hypocrite Oath
Location: It's Universal
Purpose: Furthering My Business

This might be the most predictable chapter in the entire book. It should come as no surprise to anyone that the general consensus of a great many citizens of other countries is that the average American Christian is lazy, entitled, and hypocritical. And you thought they didn't notice.

In my twenty-five years in the international coffee industry, I have heard Christians called hypocrites more times than I can count. Not really. I can count pretty high. But a lot of times.

Actually most of their opinions about Christians are formed by watching the nightly news in their country. We are linked to the actions of our society. The threshold for what is considered news doesn't vary much from country to country. Their media focus on the worst expressions of the things they oppose the most. It's understandable. At least from the news agencies that are not government controlled. Those are even more disparaging of America and its Judeo-Christian heritage. Every violent protest, mass murder, or police shooting is portrayed in such a way that the viewers in other countries can come away with the idea that the streets of America are still the Wild West. During the May Day riots in Seattle, I had concerned business colleagues in other countries call me to make sure my family and I were safe. I've learned to live with this initial perception in the countries I've been to and to be particularly sensitive in the beginning of any relationship.

Because I won't hide my faith, I know going in what I need to overcome.

To be fair, I also usually have preconceived notions about people from other countries, their faith or lack thereof, and their government. I work very hard at extending a clean slate when going into a country and meeting its people. But I'm not perfect at it. Nature hates a vacuum and so does the perception lobe of my brain. Sometimes I'm the only one with a predominantly open mind, and that's okay. I'm just fine with letting my love and acceptance of them turn the tide of the relationship. Sometimes the transition is quick and enjoyable. Sometimes it is glacial and hard-fought. No matter the duration, I have always enjoyed breaking down the walls of distrust.

Not So Different

At the end of the day though, I've discovered that people are mostly just people. When you strip away all the suspicion, perceptions, and politics, the majority of people in other countries are no different than you or I. No matter what language we speak, we all laugh in the same dialect. We Americans just happen to be citizens of a superpower that has a Judeo-Christian heritage. In spite of all the evidence to the contrary, America is still perceived as a Christian nation by the citizens of other countries. Because of that association, the conclusion of many people around the world is that Christians are hypocrites. If you're an American Christian, you're a hypocrite. Don't deny it. Everybody already knows.

In my younger days, that accusation used to irritate the snot out of me. A lot. Especially when, with no prior knowledge or relationship, it was directed at me personally. During those times I never officially considered cannibalism, but most everything else unkind entered my mind. But these same things are not as personal to me now as they once were. I like the feeling of resigned calm.

What changed? A couple of things.

First, I came to the conclusion that the only time I would allow that accusation to give me pause was if the person saying it had firsthand knowledge and experience of who I was at my core. Second, I realized that the things that torqued me the most were usually the ones that were true. Even if I didn't like it to be true. And that's not always a bad thing. Sometimes it's the very best thing.

Did I just admit to being a hypocrite? Yes. Yes, I did. Even though the word is improperly used in most cases, I know what they mean by it and I agree with the accusation. But just to poke a little fun at my editor, here is how Merriam-Webster defines the word *hypocrite*: "A person who claims or pretends to have certain beliefs about what is right but who behaves in a way that disagrees with those beliefs."

The word *hypocrite* is from the old French or late Latin and classically refers to an actor. It describes a person who convincingly plays a role that is completely at odds with who they actually are or what they actually believe.

Pretend to be a Christian? Who would do that? It's not like claiming to be a Christian carries the same social status as being an astronaut, professional athlete, marine biologist, or architect. From a standpoint of verbal abuse, pretending to be a Christian would clock in right above slumlord and just below career politician on my personal list of desirable identities. It makes no sense to pretend to be a Christian unless one craves slander or social slights.

Transparency Moment

I don't find the worldview of Christianity particularly desirable. At all. Seriously. Of all the worldviews in all the world, Christianity is the least attractive for a guy like me. I'd much prefer an esoteric, mystical romp through a field of feel-good heather. You know, saying things that sound loving and nurturing but stripping away any real accountability to make it easier. Or how about no moral absolutes? I'm in! How fun would that be! Obedience is not a life meadow I enjoy frolicking in. Sacrifice? Yuck. Dying to self? I'm trying to cut down. Unconditional love? Too much work. Praying for and loving my enemies? How about . . . um, no.

Why would I even consider announcing that I'm a follower of Jesus Christ unless I truly am? Frankly, I don't need the abuse. If I were not certain of the rightness of my beliefs, I would have tapped out of the Redeemer octagon years ago. I see almost no upside to the claim. I did not choose this Christian life. I chose Jesus Christ. The rest of it wasn't so optional.

Hello World, You Win

So, for the sake of this chapter and the point I'm making, I choose to ignore the improper use of the word *hypocrite* and focus on what is meant by the people who use it. Right here. Right now. I want to own the title *hypocrite*. I want to concede the point. I'm a hypocrite. Isn't this fun? Here—have a donut.

Anchovy Milk Shakes

What's worse: confessing our failure or resigning to a life with no standards? Easy answer, but not a fun one. For me? I would rather repeatedly fail while trying to live a life of obedience to God's Word than pretending such a standard doesn't exist. Standing for nothing is easy. Using the failures of others to justify a life lived in the margins is gutless. Taking a stand for something eternal and significant will always lead to criticism. The only real question is how will you and I respond to the criticism. Will we throw in the towel and settle into a life of spiritual mediocrity so as not to draw attention to ourselves?

Christians are not the only ones who don't live up to what they profess. Far from it. My travels have afforded me the knowledge and experience that every person of every faith, to greater and lesser degrees, is a hypocrite. Nobody, and I mean nobody, lives a life that consistently confirms their own belief system—even the critics of Christianity. Some just set the bar so low their contradictions are not so obvious. They can't argue against the merits of Christianity, only the flawed application of it. How embarrassingly weak. Nevertheless, I say, embrace the insult! It means we serve a big God. Let the critics accuse but don't allow them to have such power in your life. If you wither from the attack, the accusation will come back up as often as an anchovy milk shake. If you shrug it off and keep moving, the critics lose their desired result. They want you to say that you were wrong about this whole Jesus obsession thing. Don't let them mock you into silence or surrender. Failure will always be part of the process and nobody is exempt.

Hypocrisy is an absolute certainty. Until Jesus comes back or we become an all-you-can-eat worm buffet, we will be hypocrites. It's not a badge of honor to be worn proudly, but neither is it a thing that should shame us to silence or cause us to wither. It's our unavoidable condition.

You might also be amazed at how disarming it is to own it. Conceding the point is the perfect segue to discussing the unfathomable glory and righteousness of the God you serve.

I Fail, to Realize

Apathy is not a calling. Cynicism is not a virtue. Criticism is not instruction, and ridicule does not inspire. Understand that when people accuse you of being a hypocrite, they are just trying to verbally lessen the contrast between what you profess and how they choose to live. Seeing it for what it is can be freeing and, honestly, a bit entertaining. Often times the accusation speaks far more about their ethical cowardice than it does about our failure. We fail, but we're not failing. I'm a hypocrite. So are you. A loved, redeemed, and forgiven hypocrite. And I can't think of a better place to be.

Join me in my quest to stay the course, no matter how others perceive the sincerity of our relationship with God. Once we get comfortable with the reality that we will never fully live up to what we profess, we'll begin to get a tiny glimpse of exactly how majestic God is. It's the way of the warrior. Only the ethically blind can't recognize and acknowledge their own duplicity.

Failure won't make me back down. Blowing it helps me come to grips with my need for a savior. If God is satisfied with the covering provided by the death of his Son, who am I to question it? Sure, if I could consistently reflect the actions, commands, or desires of God, life would be so much easier—but he'd be an embarrassingly weak God. I cannot commit my entire life to a being that I can consistently reflect. If I can accurately portray him, he is not worthy of my praise and worship.

Last Thing

I love grace more than I can convey. I'd be lost without it. When I don't reflect the wishes of my Father in heaven, I will repent, hold my head high, and walk on.

But grace isn't an excuse for me to bleed my casual sin all over those around me. Based on my acknowledgment of the monumental sacrifice that was made on my behalf, grace should be the tourniquet that stems the flow of my unholy activity.

We on the same page? (When you think about it, that was kind of funny. I'm just saying.)

Be a bard. A bard for Jesus. Admit to being a hypocrite. Hail the fail. Embrace the grace. (Cue fans of the movie *The Princess Bride*. "No more rhymes now! I mean it." . . .)

·············· *Shun Common* ··

Chapter: Typecasting Our Nets

Location: Guatemala City, Guatemala

Purpose: Sourcing Coffee

I was in Guatemala City, Guatemala—a poor capital city in a poor country in a region of exceedingly poor countries. I wasn't lost again but I was definitely flummoxed. I had just gotten back from a trip to the countryside to see some coffee-growing operations. In the midst of the coffee fields sat a small village comprised of the people who worked this land.

Note: We passed several semi-active volcanoes on the way to the village. Really enjoyed my potential Pompeii moment.

My guides dutifully answered my run-of-the-mill questions but stared at me like I was a different species. Did they think I was fabulously wealthy? I wasn't. Were they trying to imagine what my life was like? If so, my life obviously appeared more interesting from the outside than it was in reality. Whatever the reasons, I was clearly an anomaly to them. But I just wanted to be their friend. I wanted them to know if you strip away the superficial junk, I was just like them. I felt like I should eat a plantain and pee in a bush so they'd know my body operates on the same basic principles as theirs do.

It was the weekend and people were milling about this little village and staring at me as well. I wished I were better looking. Oversight by God, I'm pretty sure. A lot of young adults just hung out around old rusted-out cars or small clusters of trees. Nobody in these groups seemed to be doing anything other than staring at me. Did I have food on my face or look like an ancient Mayan prince? Unlikely . . . at least the latter. I was escorted around the decrepit coffee processing facilities and dilapidated warehouses. I nodded and smiled a lot.

On the way back to our vehicle, I saw the same young people standing in the same places. I asked my guide, "Why do they just stand there?"

His answer messed up my relative calm. He explained that they were anticipating the next group of Christians that was scheduled to arrive soon.

What?

"How often do Christians come here to help?" I asked.

"Fairly regularly," was the response. "This village is not as dependent on the American church as some villages are. Some villages in the region do very little except wait for the next church group to come down and give them something."

It felt like I had pulled my heart muscle. Not because I saw these people as lazy or shiftless but because of the unintended consequences of Western benevolence, including mine. What are we doing? What was I doing?

Let me explain what made my heart hurt so much and what I realized we might be doing wrong.

The All-Too-Common Church Missions Program

· Round up a dozen or so zealous souls from the congregation.
· Gather clothes, functional items, building materials, tools, and Bibles.
· Book a flight to Mexico, Central America, or South America.
· Do the Lord's work.

The motivation? Commendable. At least it seems to be. The Lord's work? Maybe, but it's certainly not the best kind of work available if we are to call it "missions." These mission trips might change the lives of the people going, but what about the people they're claiming to help? I believe it can be dehumanizing. Here's why.

Like a perpetual welfare recipient, these villages have adopted the idea that they are incapable of a sustainable life, and we reinforce this idea with material makeovers and backslapping encouragement. Providing only a handout will ensure that the next time we're there, their same hand will be out too. No activity is more spiritually depleting than being given perpetual donations and praise with no real solution for reversing the fundamental reasons for the poverty.

I'm not saying that providing temporary assistance, friendship, food, clothing, or facilities is a bad thing. I do that when the opportunity presents itself. But if that's all we do for these people, we are treating a broken leg with an ice-cream cone, a wink, and a smile. They will feel better for a few moments, but that cone isn't going to get them walking again.

Remember the old adage about teaching a man to fish rather than giving him a fish? We need to give people like these Guatemalan villagers even more. We need to teach them how to make the fishing poles. I may provide a wholesale opportunity for them to sell their coffee, but since they don't own the land, they're getting the same pennies on the dollar they would get for selling their coffee to any other source.

Now I was staring at me too. I didn't like what I saw.

God had allowed me to see the inside of this village refrigerator after the door was closed, and it was dark and cold. Most of us only see these villages when they're wide open and expecting us. I was seeing them in between the waves of Americans. What had we done?

Transform the Norm

I have wondered: What if the money we're pouring into short-term mission trips was funneled into interest-free loans for land purchases instead? The communities could then work the land and receive the lion's share of the profits for their efforts instead of sharecropping for next to nothing. In time, they would make enough money to pay off the loan for the land.

Paying the land off by their own hard work would involve them in the process. It would give them skin in the game. People hold high value on what they have sacrificed to attain. Land ownership trumps ethnic heritage, bigotry, and formal education.

If that were too involved or not economically viable for churches or individuals, wouldn't it be better if we brought an agronomist on the mission trip who could help the community double or triple the yield of their crops?

What about forming a cooperative to combine the community's buying power with other villages, in order to receive the best prices for their seeds and crops?

But maybe others in the community have no vocation at all? Fine. Provide micro-business loans and help them start developing income outside of the village. Am I making sense?

There are amazing organizations already doing stuff like this: World Concern, Agros International, and Kiva, to name a few. Don't worry, there's plenty of room and destitution for more people to engage. Granted, it is not as easy as just going down and slapping up a cinderblock cathedral, but shouldn't the goal be to help them out of their poverty permanently?

I can get creative. You can too, I know it. Can we imagine other ways to change a community's station in life and not just give them a shiny new building to celebrate their systemic poverty? If those we seek to help are involved in the process of their economic restoration, spirits are transformed and God is seriously glorified.

Too Much Candy

Do you remember the actor John Candy? Many remember him as Uncle Buck, the shower curtain ring salesman in *Planes, Trains and Automobiles*, or Tom Hanks's on-screen brother in *Splash*. He was truly hilarious. He was also a large man and died way too young. He was stellar at playing the hapless, lazy, irresponsible, gregarious, and slovenly goof. He had an infectious personality and was a unique force in entertainment. But he was tragically typecast. If he lost weight, he wouldn't be John Candy. If he stayed large, he would have consistent work and acclaim but would likely die at an early age.

Imagine being John Candy. You have to choose between fame and fortune that could kill you far too soon, or the death of your dream of acting so you could live a longer life. Which path would you choose?

Reboot Our Programs

We can't allow our missional efforts to be typecast into roles that, like John Candy, will result in their premature death. Let's wean ourselves, our business models, and our congregations off the easy displays of spiritual philanthropy and instead focus our efforts on assisting people out of their systemic despair, permanently. Let's not settle for the obvious roles, the easy or traditional missional roles. We need to take on the hard scripts. The challenging ones. The ones that max our abilities to the breaking point.

Giving is easy. Coming alongside people for the long haul is hard. The process of restoration has always been hard-fought.

Sowing an understanding in our actions and not just our words that God sees these communities as capable requires more of us than just showing up and playing the same basic character, over and over again. That type of missional effort will not survive for any real length of time. Let's make peers, not dependent, adoring fans.

We (and we includes me) need to engage in the type of effort that sustains people, builds families, establishes communities, and endures for generations, at home and abroad.

Anything less is a type of welfare that leaves the imbalance of opportunity as one-sided as it was when we arrived. How can that possibly be considered missions? Benevolence, or charity maybe, but not truly missions. I had to rethink my business protocols, and I did.

It's a Good Grind

If all we seek is to feel good and make a few friends, stay the course. But my gut tells me we're sending the wrong message. Our missional efforts can be fat, popular, and short-lived, or they can be disciplined, empowering, and enduring. We need to stop being satisfied with just providing (John) Candy-grams to the poor. It doesn't work. And neither will the people receiving them, if that's all we provide.

············ *Shun Common* ·······································

Chapter: Obviously Ambiguous

Location: Osaka, Japan

Purpose: Hiring Staff

Osaka, Japan, is an interesting city. The language of the people there is not considered as sophisticated as their Tokyo counterparts. Me? I could hear only subtle differences. Even with the perceived lack of spoken refinement, the Osaka-ben, as it's called, is still stuffed with nuance and subtlety—like all Japanese dialects.

So many ways to say the word "no" depending on the social situation. They might say "yes" to a direct question, but that doesn't necessarily mean "yes." Sometimes they say a "yes" that really means "no" so as not to embarrass the individual. They all understand what's being said just fine. To this American, it can get confusing. And confused I got.

I recall one particular business meeting that seemed to be going quite well. At the point I thought it was appropriate, I solicited a very direct response as to their company's acceptance of my business proposal. To my utter delight, they said yes. I thought I had nailed it! For the remainder of the meeting I bounced in my chair and grinned at all of them like we were long-lost soul mates. All of which multiplied my utter embarrassment when my Japanese business partner broke their real response to me after the meeting was over. The yes was actually a no. I looked at him and thought an elbow in the ribs or a kick to the shin under the table would have been better than allowing me to carry on like a giddy buffoon. But my Japanese friend was even too polite to do that. The "yes" they responded with was meant to protect me from losing face. I sure showed them. When it came to the art of face losing, I didn't require anyone's help. (I try not to hang on to this type of stuff, but my clueless euphoria in that meeting still haunts me a little.)

In my house, that word is "maybe."

To this day, I find this type of linguistic nuance confusing and, in that particular instance, humiliating.

I Like the Word *Flummoxed*

The Bible has always struck me the same way. It can confuse me. (If I didn't know better, I would think God enjoys seeing me flummoxed.) For example, in the first chapter of the gospel of John, we read, "In the beginning was the Word, and the Word was with God, and the Word was God." Now seriously, what's with this cryptic language? How hard would it be to throw us a head-slappingly obvious bone here! Why couldn't John just say, "In the beginning was Jesus, and Jesus was with God, and Jesus was God"? Is this scriptural sudoku?

I've yet to meet a person who accepted Jesus as Savior based on their desperate need for ambiguity. So let's unwrap this puppy just a little bit and see if it's really the savior subterfuge it appears to be.

Questions for the Word

In Luke, chapter 7, John the Baptist dispatches a couple of members of his entourage to ask Jesus a question. They tell Jesus, "John the Baptist sent us to you to ask, 'Are you the one who is to come, or should we expect someone else?'"

They ask this question smack-dab in a time when Jesus has been churning out miracles like personality quirks in a junior high youth group. Right here, I just want Jesus to say, "Yep, I'm the guy you've been waiting for, so rest easy and tell your boss I'm sending a new swarm of locust his way—bon appétit."

He doesn't. Jesus, being quintessentially Jesus, answers their question with an abbreviated version of his current résumé. I usually find it irritating when someone answers a straightforward character question by reciting his or her credentials. When Jesus does it, though, it always cuts straight to the very heart of our hearts.

He says, "Report to John what you have seen and heard: The blind receive sight, the lame walk, those who have leprosy are cleansed, the deaf hear, the dead are raised, and the good news is proclaimed to the poor."

He puts it back on them. Not because he can't answer the question. He does it because the conclusion should be inescapable. I also believe he does this because God delights in engaging us in the discovery of him. But unlike understanding the subtle, social dance of the Japanese language, God isn't the least bit interested in the preservation of my pride. Both the Japanese language and Scripture challenge me to seek, discover, and learn, but only the language of God truly has my best interest at heart.

The Game We All Played

Ever play hide-and-seek as a kid? Scratch that question. I know you did. Which was more fun, being found or finding the kid hiding? I don't know why I even asked that question. Obviously, finding the kid hiding was *way* more fun. Unless the kid was too easy to find. Then it felt like you'd been robbed of some anticipated elation.

We were created to seek. Curiosity is a sacred calling and part of our very makeup. Curiosity may have mercifully killed the cat, but unless we're curious about the right things, curiosity can reduce us to hamster-wheel-bound zombies. And tragically, some people advance no further than merely being curious about what it's like to be curious about God.

I'm curious about scads of things. You too? I've known women who seem curious about how many pairs of shoes they'd need to own to make a centipede blush. I've known men who, regardless of the frequency of rejection, are convinced that somewhere in the world a supermodel is looking for a guy exactly like them. (With men, the line between curiosity and delusion can get a little slender.) *Ha!*

The fact is many of us spend a great deal of our life's energy applying pointless ointment to our natural curiosity and hoping it will salve the condition. Too often we look for all the wrong things. And when we do, we arrive at all the wrong conclusions.

Silence Is Golden

Once I was able to own the humiliation of my wrong conclusion in that Japanese meeting, I was able to learn two significant things about language and life in Osaka, Japan.

First, there is no such thing as an uncomfortable silence. If you're uncomfortable, that's on you. Had I remained silent and just let the meeting play out, I would not have pushed them into the "yes means no" corner. The Japanese do not feel compelled to fill in every conversational gap during a business negotiation or casual conversation. It's perfectly acceptable for half a dozen people to sit around a table and, in the midst of a given topic, not speak for a minute or two. If they're asked a question they haven't considered, they'll process their thoughts before they respond. Me? I like to think on the fly. I formulate my opinion as I prattle on. It obviously wasn't always effective over there. The Japanese way is actually quite peaceful once you get used to it.

Second, international business contracts are almost always done in English. It's a straightforward language with little nuance. It's coarse and direct. The Japanese refer to English as "the language of lawyers." They think it's much better suited for the clarity required in complex agreements.

Both lessons have been invaluable to me over the years. Being comfortable with a prolonged silence in a group setting has taught me how to be still and quiet before God. I think God likes it when I'm still and quiet before him. Come to think of it, everyone else seems to prefer me that way as well.

But the most important thing I took away from these experiences was that God's Word is not just for me. It's not just for Americans—or lawyers! The Word of God belongs to the world. The language of the Bible is crafted for everyone. If it's not as direct in some places as you'd like, get over it. I sure needed to. Jesus wasn't American. He's a big God and it's a big world. Some people need the nuance and complexity. It's how they think, relate, and talk. I love the idea that God's Word is universal in its ability to engage the reader and speak to the heart of anyone on any level. How amazing is that?

How much easier would it have been if Jesus had been direct with his responses? I think much easier. For me. But I don't believe it would have been nearly as effective for people of other cultures. God's Word strikes a perfect balance between God being obvious and being too complex to understand without us seeking and discovering him. His Word compels us to pursue and drives us to uncover the riches. Anything too obvious and the discovery would not captivate some.

Proverbs 25:2 says, "It is the glory of God to conceal a matter; to search out a matter is the glory of kings."

The Good News Juice

If the Bible were a fruit and we put it into a press to squeeze out the contents, the juice would taste like the perfect balance of humility and love, mystery and straightforward admonitions—and the flavor would be delicious to every person on earth. If only they'd drink.

God's phrasing calls us out and challenges us to unearth the riches of his nature. The phrasing of his Word is intentional and, if we'll engage, it will draw us into a lifelong dance of mystery, discovery, awe, and fascination. His Word is exactly how it should be—for everyone. Press in, and press out the juice, my friend.

············ Shun Common ·······································

Chapter: His Grapes, My Wrath
Location: Mexico City, Mexico
Purpose: Training Classes

Mexico City is large. I am talking humongous. (I had to look up how to spell that.) Sure, it's not as imposing as some other cities and the structures feel less antiseptic. I think I find stucco soothing. But the size? Whoa. It's a mass of humanity that very few cities in the world can compare to.

My corporate guides are knowledgeable and fun. I feel welcomed and taken care of. I've been here before, but this time I feel more in tune with the people and the culture. But in the midst of all that in-tune-ness, I recognized something.

I'm not Mexican and never will be.

Big revelation, huh? No seriously, think about it. I could move to Mexico City. I could learn the language fluently. I could learn the history, customs, honorifics, spice palette, political system, and important holidays. I could obtain permanent residency and then citizenship. I could raise a family there and have every important relationship in my life be a by-product of my living in Mexico. I could pour all I am and do into the country of Mexico.

Do you know what that would make me? A citizen of Mexico. But I would never be Mexican. Is that a bad thing? No. It's just a thing. Subtle distinction? Yes, but an important one. Being a citizen of Mexico is about legal status. Being Mexican, like being Chinese or Moroccan, is about ethnicity.

Infinitesimally small differences in my DNA will forever exclude me from being Mexican, no matter how sincere my desire to live in Mexico might be.

My Dumb Germinates

Christians have a similar feeling when it comes to who qualifies as one of their own. Not all of us, mind you, but more than we'd care to admit.

In the United States, and in every place I've ever traveled, people do horrific things to other people. It's our collective condition. Every now and then, some whacked-out psycho commits an atrocity so vile I can't imagine how anyone could do such a thing to another person. I'm not talking about crimes of passion, gang-related turf wars, serving haggis to a loved one, or a drug-deal-gone-bad type of murder. I mean the real reprehensible type of crime that's as useful to society as boy bands or malaria. HA

When I watched the news stories about these psychos, I'd become convinced I was completely superior to such people. I'd get all puffy-headed about it. I'd feel certain God must be so glowingly tickled with me that he could scarcely contain his chest-swelling pride. How could he not be? I'd never do anything that deplorable!

Usually my feelings of revulsion and superiority subsided over time. Then at some point I'd intentionally forget these people. I wrote them off. Society's macabre fascination with them was akin to how they view lab rats. Then they'd disappear from our collective memory. Do I ever pray for them? To my shame, almost never.

Then out of nowhere, sometimes years later, the same vile people are again thrust into the limelight on TV, or in *People* magazine, or at the end of an IV drip. Their sudden reemergence in the public eye usually signifies the conclusion of their trial and the beginning of their life sentence, or in some cases the carrying out of their death sentence.

Don't Say That!

I used to shake my head in disgust when they'd interview these criminals. I knew how it would go. Wearing my best grumpy-bucket scowl, I'd wait for the phrase to sputter out of the criminal's mouth—the words that make nonbelievers scoff and believers fume. Whether it's Jeffrey Dahmer or Sean Sellers, these same people who committed unspeakable acts against their fellow humans talk about their conversion experience, profess their faith in Jesus Christ, and confidently claim God's forgiveness. What the stink just happened? Apparently, I'd become indignant and thoroughly convinced that a flame-resistant pair of salvation knickers should never be extended to people like them. Because of their crimes, I was comfortable seeing them only as the callous animals they were when I first learned of them.

Sound familiar?

I'm so two-faced. And I always seem to pick the uglier one of the two.

Why My Holier-Than-Thou Britches Get All Bunched Up

There are things in this life that work me into a rabid lather for no other reason than to mollify my own misguided sense of self and fairness. No excuses. It's just what I do!

First, I'm good at imagining my pre-salvation life provided a much clearer runway for the Jesus plane to safely land on, rather than that of a heinous criminal.

Second, I'm often not altogether pleased with the way God dispenses love and mercy.

My inability to get past the first one should be too embarrassing to comment extensively on. It's the equivalent of Lizzie Borden demanding to be acquitted because, prior to hacking her parents to death, she had for years kissed them on the cheek each night before going to bed. Yes, I know she was acquitted. But, come on, so was O. J.

Our pre-salvation condition always confirms our need for Jesus—it never invalidates it. Nothing we have done or not done merits greater consideration in the redemption of our souls. God draws and calls those whom he pleases in the time frame and manner that he alone sees as fit.

The second reason my britches would get all bunched up has a lot to do with the way I respond to the parables of Christ. I'm at ease with parables . . . as long as they're only applied to the exact circumstance they were given in. Once outside of that immediate context—like when they're applied to other areas of my life—I feel they should be subject to my wise and sound judgment.

Shocker: I realize God might feel otherwise.

An Example

In the first half of Matthew 20, Jesus tells a parable about a vineyard owner. The owner hires a number of workers early in the morning and agrees to pay them a set amount. They accept and begin to work. He keeps contracting workers throughout the day and hires the final group only one hour before the end of the workday.

When all the workers assemble to be paid at the end of the day, some become angry that the ones who only worked one hour were paid the same as everyone else. Even though they had agreed to the wage, they now felt ripped off. Instead of rejoicing in the work and the fair wage they were given, they could not see past the perceived injustice.

This, like almost everything Christ said, reaches beyond the obvious and brings the light of truth to other areas—even to the areas I find chair-squirmingly uncomfortable.

Not My Call

The parable of the generous vineyard owner forces me to concede that forgiveness is not mine to determine. Justice is not mine to impose, and worth is not mine to quantify. I need to get out of the business of rendering determinations about what is merited and what is not when it comes to the judgment or mercy of God.

From this vantage point, I am forced to admit I am no more or less worthy of my salvation than the worst of the worst here on earth. I also become keenly aware that my salvation is not enhanced or legitimized over time. I do not become more or less deserving of salvation based on the point in time in which I invoke it. God does not need my approval to call anyone else his own at any point he desires.

Jesus says the owner of the vineyard responds to one of the disgruntled workers this way: "I am not being unfair to you, friend. Didn't you agree to work for a denarius? Take your pay and go. I want to give the one who was hired last the same as I gave you. Don't I have the right to do what I want with my own money? Or are you envious because I am generous?"

I have no right to be envious or angry about the generosity of God. I

need to get out of the indignation business when it comes to the transformation of others. Who am I to question such things? God is God
and has the right to do as he pleases with his eternal currency. If a
criminal proclaims the name of Jesus, I need to rejoice as if it's one-
hundred-percent true. If it's not, God will sort it out. It's not in my job
description.

Not a Lick of Difference

Even with all its faults (and there are at least two or three), America
has some really cool things about it. Here's one: imagine that one of
the people I spent time with in Mexico City came to the United States
to live and work. Let's say they learned the language, learned about our
history, customs, political system, and holidays. Then they took the test
and oath of citizenship.

Do you know what that would make them? American. As American
as me. I mean, they can't become president, but by the letter of the law
there shouldn't be any difference between me and that freshly sworn-in
citizen. I realize that the application of that is not always as it should
be and that, as a country, we've strayed so far from the truth. People
are so tribal. But the principle, the ideal, the intention is beautiful and
right.

As a country, we have lost our way. As the body of Christ, we can't
afford that. We need to unabashedly be like America's supposed to be.
Without judgment or hesitation. If Jack the Ripper, at the end of his bar-
baric murder spree, had repented and genuinely accepted Jesus, do you
know what that would make him? A Christian. Worthy of eternal com-
munion with God. And it doesn't make a lick of difference if I approve
of it or not. Nor should it.

The history of a person has absolutely no bearing on the authenticity of their salvation. If they have truly repented and taken and passed
the Jesus-acceptance exam, they are clean and right before God. Even
the worst of the worst. And at the end of the day, we're all the worst
of the worst. From the second God transforms their hearts, they are
exactly the same as me. A full-fledged citizen of heaven.

Nobody's Been Shortchanged

I agreed to the terms of my salvation, and it was more compensation than I should have ever received.

Saying "I deserve the death penalty" is easy. Truly knowing this demands a whole new level of personal surrender from me. God has been way more than fair with me. As promised, I received my salvation denarius. My inability to grasp his immense holiness and compassion is not an excuse to debate the individual salvation qualifications of others. It's no slight to me if anyone else is given the same privilege of proclaiming Jesus as Lord and Savior, even if that proclamation is uttered with their final breath. I require a merciful and loving pardon from God as much as anyone else on the planet.

I need to own this. Every. Single. Day.

Shun Common

Chapter: A Tale of Two Pities

Location: Barranquilla, Colombia

Purpose: Expansion Talks

CliffsNotes of a well-known story: he heard, he ran, the wind blew, the seas raged, he went swimming, big fishy swallowed, God fetched, and the plot thickened. Sound familiar? You guessed it. Jonah. And the gonzo fish. Or whale. Doesn't matter much for this chapter. (Unless you're a marine biologist and sensitive to these matters. To you, my deep apologies.) On second thought, let's go with whale. Whew. No hate mail from people way smarter than me.

Eventually the hero of the story was puked up on the shore and decided God was not going to allow him to run from this particular gig. (Jonah might have also been a little thankful that God chose regurgitation as opposed to the alternative exit point.) In any case, sporting a fresh sheen of aqua-slobber, Jonah took to the streets of Nineveh. He did as God instructed and told the citizens they needed to turn from their evil ways or God would destroy them and the city. Not exactly a Hallmark moment.

Now mind you, Nineveh was not a remote caravan pit stop. The Bible says it was an extremely important city of about 120,000 people. Jonah went throughout the city preaching that the people needed to repent and serve God. Amazingly the people heard the warning and did as God instructed them through Jonah. They repented and God's anger was turned away.

I wonder if some of the people were influenced when they saw him get spit out by a whale. Me? If a guy came flying out of the mouth of a whale and started telling me to repent, he would have my rapt attention the instant my jaw stopped bumping my belly button. And I'd give serious consideration to the words he spoke.

The people of Nineveh apparently felt the same. In spite of a few militant Greenpeace members who were bused in to protest the message, the people responded and God spared the city.

There's an element in the story that yells my name—one of those beyond-obvious things that keeps poking its hand into the sky like a first grader with a full bladder. Although it has nothing to do with Jonah's gastric mode of transport.

It has to do with how Jonah responded to the repentance of the people. Feels like how I might respond.

Oh, who am I kidding? Might? No might. It's a definite.

The number of times I've lamented my actions because of how the end result made me look couldn't be counted on an abacus. I've sat right on that hillside with Jonah, moaning, "Now, Lord, take away my life, for it is better for me to die than to live." We know Jonah was also angry that God had spared the city, but seriously angry people want to take someone else's life, not have God take theirs. What really seems to be eating his kosher corndog is that his prophet cred is now under citywide investigation. Why else would he ask God to take away his life?

Parrot Tossing

I always desire to do the right thing. I want to be seen as compassionate. Sensitive. But sometimes, no matter how hard I try, it just doesn't work out that way. One instance stands out when it comes to me desiring to do the right thing. It involved a parrot—yes, another stinking parrot. Of all my stories of my missteps, I feel like I'm supposed to use this one for this chapter. Go figure.

I was invited to a business associate's house who lived in the beautiful port city of Barranquilla, Colombia. We had a wonderful traditional Colombian dinner (translation of my nebulous description: I can't actually recall what they served me!) after which we settled down to talk business. We sat in his living room and his wife and children joined us. They had a gigantic white parrot that the children tormented relentlessly. It took a while for me to feel badly for the hydraulic poop machine, but somehow I did.

Then I had an idea! I asked if I could hold the bird. I would show them what a compassionate and kindhearted fellow I was. This would be the moment when they realized that I was different, and then I would have the opportunity to tell them why. How could this possibly fail?

My host said, "Of course, but allow me to caution you: our feathered friend here can be quite surly."

I listened but didn't hear. I had a plan. I was supposed to hold the parrot. Given the way the family treated him, I was certain the bird would appreciate my kindness. I felt like God was instructing me to show my hosts what a wonderfully genuine guy they were dealing with here.

"But I don't like parrots, God." I told him. "You know that."

"I've got your back," was the response I got.

I think.

Slowly, so as not to startle the beast, I eased over and put my hand out. To my surprise, the parrot stepped lightly onto my extended hand. As I sat back down, I talked soothingly to the bird to let him know I was a friend. I stroked his head and smiled inside at the brilliance of my plan. He seemed so content. Feathers flat. So far, so good. I had this. I was a parrot whisperer!

The bird sat peacefully for the first minute or so. Just long enough to lull me into a false sense of accomplishment. Then he turned his head and looked at me. What was that look for?

In what I can only describe as a slow-motion assault, he casually lowered his head, eyes never leaving mine, and clamped onto my index finger. His eyes still on me, he ramped up the beak pressure. It took me a second to grasp what was happening. Why would he bite me? I was the only one in the room not harassing the snot out of him!

By the time I realized this bird was looking to do serious damage, it was too late. He was locked on and loving it. The pain came front and center quite suddenly. I freaked . . . just a little. I flung out my arm and, with it, the bird. My sudden catapulting of the feathered assassin freaked him out as well. He went kind of . . . well, nuts.

He was flying and squawking so fast and so loud everyone in the room panicked as well. I had no idea what to do. The room was pure chaos.

Eventually the kids chased the psychotic bird down the hallway. My host and his wife just stared at me with a "way to go, Officer Overreaction" look on their faces: "We warned you."

Inside I was screaming, "What happened to that whole 'I've got your back' thing, God?"

His response? Nada.

My face flushed and my finger throbbing, we mercifully called it a night. That was the last time they invited me over to their home. Big surprise.

I later regretted my kindness toward the flying vice grip. A lot. Yes, I know it's not exactly the same emotional dynamic as Jonah was experiencing, but it's not as far off as you might imagine. In spite of my less than enthusiastic feelings about parrots, I did what I believed God was asking me to do. To show my kindness as a proof of my credibility as a businessman and a compassionate Christian—and it bit me good.

I felt betrayed. Not by the bird. I didn't trust him anyway. But by God. My best intentions had ended so badly that I felt like I had just squandered an opportunity to witness to these people. Had I? I might not ever know until I assume room temperature and stand before my Maker. At this point, I can only hope that God did something with my gesture. Jonah had shown obedience and compassion to the people of Nineveh and came away with his own perceived bite marks. And they hurt. Jonah also felt betrayed. I so dig that about Jonah.

Boiling Mad

I relate to that guy, big time. If we ever meet, I hope Jonah can relate to me even though I've never been mistaken for krill.

Back to the Jonah story. After the entire city repented and turned to God, we find Jonah sitting on the side of a hill. Once he realized God was no longer miffed at Nineveh, Jonah was miffed. Rather than rejoicing that God's warning had been heeded and 120,000 people had not been charred, deluged, or pummeled by pumas, Jonah got dramatic.

Jonah was more concerned about how their repentance made him look than he was that they were spared and had turned to serving God.

I mean, surely the entire town couldn't have repented? Why couldn't God have at least raised a few boils on them or caused someone to spontaneously combust? That way they would have known that what he warned them about had some teeth! With *all* of them spared, there was no way to verify his credibility as a prophet of God.

Now that mind-set, my friend, is a pity.

Skinless Faces

How many times have I felt the subtle but unmistakable promptings of the Father to share the gospel, but I don't do it? Lots. I concern myself with a multitude of issues that God has said, "That's not your concern!" My go-to cop-out is to respond with, "Well, I'm not really a religious man. My spiritual beliefs are strong, but they're my own." Interpretation: I'm too much of a wuss to just speak the truth as instructed and let God handle my reputation. I'm more concerned about being seen as a normal guy than I am about others hearing the good news. (And all this time I thought the crowds were chanting "More Ron!" Apparently not.)

Too often I've been embarrassed and silent about God's mercy and desire that none should perish—and all because I'm worried about how it will turn out or make me look. That, my friend, is no less a pity than Jonah's response.

Or the times when I've finally worked up the courage to share Christ only to find out that the person was already saved. No way! I've been seriously bummed by the news that they were a believer! Be honest . . . it can't just be me!

It feels like a barge-load of wasted emotion and energy. For most of us, the prospect of sharing Christ with a total stranger generates the same enthusiasm as being summoned for jury duty. The last thing any of us hopes for is to finally work up the courage to share Jesus, step off that cliff, and then be blindsided by a redeemed soul!

Rather than rejoicing with them as a fellow believer, I begin to imagine what their face would look like without skin. Okay, maybe not that extreme. But I might feel a little resentment, especially if they don't at least recognize the Herculean effort it took for me to talk to them in the first place.

Embarrassed to Death

Jonah was so ashamed of God's compassion because of how it made him look that he would have preferred to die rather than face this phantom humiliation. Like Jonah, have you ever lost sight of the big picture to the point that you would have chosen severe consequences over the potential public embarrassment? Like me, have you ever flung your own metaphorical parrot across a room, creating chaos and resentment? Is it possible for us to move beyond such a self-centered view of life, service, and circumstance? I hope so, or we're wasting way more time and energy than Jonah thought he had.

Jonah wasn't betrayed by God, and I wasn't betrayed by a parrot. Or God, for that matter. It was just a silly parrot, for goodness' sake. My actions resulted in a bruise and a pitifully small scab. Jonah's actions resulted in a bruised ego, not much else. Yes, I realize that I don't have anything in my life that's on dramatic par with saving a city and then wanting to die. So you're going to have to get what you're going to get from this chapter by way of the parrot incident. Buck up, little camper.

I'm not called to read the tea leaves of consequence. Rather than deciding what I will and will not do based on how it makes me feel and look, wouldn't it be more eternally satisfying for me to do what I was actually destined and instructed to do?

If you're keeping score at home, that's an affirmative. Life and joy are in the obedience, not the outcome. If God tells me to go tell someone about his love for them, I need to do it. If I hear God, or even think I hear God, tell me to be kind to the parrot, no matter how many lacerated appendages are in store for me, I need to pick up the hollow-boned agony machine. No questions asked. Smile and take the pain. I was warned. I knew the risk.

So did Jonah.

Shun Common

Chapter: Hello, My Name Is Esther

Location: Hackettstown, NJ

Purpose: Mailing in My Crown

The book of Esther is one of my favorites. I think I've leaned on the lessons in that book more than almost any other in the Bible. Which is kind of odd because Esther is the only book in the Bible that does not explicitly mention God. Ten chapters and the protagonist doesn't make an appearance? You'd think his name might have come up at least once. But, noooo!

You might be wondering—where's Ron going with this? How will he tie this into a coffee-related anecdote?

Simple.

I'm not going to. It was a bit of a tangent. Let's keep this one just between us, okay?

I'm still going to stay with the book of Esther but my main point has nothing to do with God not being explicitly mentioned in it.

The Early Years

In the early years of my business, money was tight and times were tough. I was scrambling just to keep my head above water. My Japanese partner and I had opened our first few coffee shops in Japan and the travel, in conjunction with the learning curve, made for some massively uncertain times. We had had just enough money, drive, and stupidity to get this far, but now we were running critically low on the first two.

Then, like seeing the lights of a distant gas station with my needle on empty, I received an inquiry from an Egyptian investment group that wanted a master licensing agreement for my brand. This was not just good news—it was great news. I moved forward with the licensing contract as quickly as possible without looking desperate. I thought I was smooth.

I didn't fool them.

Shortly after my first trip to Cairo to secure location leases, the main spokesman for the group scheduled a meeting with me. During that meeting, he made me aware that they knew I was just barely holding on financially. But they believed in me and in my coffee shop concept. So much so that they wanted to provide the working capital required for me to expand the company exponentially.

I had kept the business lean and debt free since day one. No debt was good. But no working capital? Not so much. Now this. I couldn't believe my good fortune. As smoothly and calmly as my desperation allowed, I negotiated a big lump of dough in exchange for an equity stake in my company. They accepted a minority stock position so I would still maintain control of the whole company. I thought I had just snagged the brass ring, seconds prior to me falling completely off the horse. We signed the agreement. I was stoked. I had found favor with all the right people and I was rolling.

Fast track to success, meet Ron.

Play nice and do well, you two.

This was the first time in my business life that I could have used some diet shampoo. Big head and all, I was off and running like a blow-dryer. Lots of hot air and way too noisy for its size.

The money was to be wired to my bank account in ninety days. And I had a signed contract. What could go wrong? I plowed forward as if the money was already in the bank. You can see it coming, right?

The funding day came and went. But I was assured that it would only be slightly delayed. So I kept spending and pushing forward. There were some other assurances and missed dates, but I won't drag this story out. They had lost a court case that they had been all but assured of winning, and the loss had completely decimated their financial position. They would need at least a year to recover financially. It would be tough sledding for a while, but they had a plan. Their company would survive. Their biggest problem just then was me. I had a legally binding contract.

(Dramatic pause . . .) It was high-tension stuff indeed. I had never had this kind of power before. I didn't like the feeling or the reality of it.

Neither did Esther. She had her own rock-and-a-hard-place conundrum to figure out.

First Esther

Esther was a woman whose parents had died and who was watched over by her cousin Mordecai. The Bible says that Esther had exceeding beauty in appearance and form.

My Bible doesn't have pictures in it, but based on the text, it seems Esther was relatively easy on the iris.

The king of Persia during that time was Xerxes and the queen's name was Vashti. After being summoned by the king to provide eye candy for his friends, Queen Vashti refused to come and the king became angry. Xerxes already had some anger management issues. According to one Greek historian, he once had a river whipped for disobeying him. (Obviously, not a go-with-the-flow type fellow.) As a consequence of Vashti's disobedience, the king banished her from ever being in his presence again.

The king's love brokers determined that a replacement should be found for her. They searched the land and brought many candidates to the royal palace. It was like *The Bachelor* on steroids. Esther was chosen to be one of them, but Mordecai instructed her not to reveal her nationality. Esther was Hebrew. A Jew. Let's just say anti-Semitism wasn't a modern invention. So she heeded his words and remained mum on her ethnic identity. And eventually, after her night in King Xerxes's love tent, she was selected as queen of Persia. Mordecai continued to watch over Esther from a distance and on occasion spoke with her. Esther had found amazing favor with the king and her influence was immense.

About this time a vile little weasel named Haman was also appointed to a position of considerable authority. People were supposed to kneel down to Haman when he passed by, which is why the guards confronted Mordecai at the king's gate when he refused to pay Haman honor. Mordecai told them he was a Jew. Enough said, I guess.

Haman got all red-eye about the snub and began the process of issuing an edict. An edict that any Jew throughout the kingdom was to be killed. Just like that. A time was appointed for the carrying out of the edict, as was the custom of the day.

As the date approached, Esther sent a servant to Mordecai to find out what was going on. Mordecai told her all that he knew of the edict and the impending annihilation of the Jews. Not necessarily a pleasant family moment. Mordecai implored Esther to use her influence with the king to save the Jews, but Esther balked at this notion and instead cited the peril she would face if she did. Not only was it certain death for anyone who approached the king without being summoned—he finished near the bottom of his sensitivity training class—but she herself was a Jew.

Mordecai called her out. In Esther 4, he responded with something less than warm fire and a cup of tea: "Do not think that because you are in the king's house you alone of all the Jews will escape. For if you remain silent at this time, relief and deliverance for the Jews will arise from another place, but you and your father's family will perish. And who knows but that you have come to your royal position for such a time as this?"

In spite of her personal peril, Esther decided to take the risk and approach the king on behalf of the Jews.

What happened next? Stay tuned . . .

Now for Me

I had a legally binding contract. I wasn't accustomed to living in the lap of luxury like Esther must have been, but I was growing exceedingly fond of the idea. The Egyptian investment group may not have had the liquid cash to honor our agreement, but they certainly had enough assets to make this right by me. I told myself that I had come too far to turn back now. In reality, I had told too many people how I was going to knock this business out of the park with my newfound business wealth. Like Esther, I was feeling pretty good about my place in life, and the idea of giving it up was not one I wanted to entertain. I had made too many business promises and plans to survive if this money didn't come through. Unlike Esther, I wasn't risking physical death—but the almost certain demise of my company was front and center in my mind.

I was trying to come up with any idea with these guys that would keep this deal alive. They balked at everything. There was simply no way they could fulfill their contract to me.

My option?

Litigation. Litigation that would absolutely end up in my favor. That idea wasn't acceptable to me. It wasn't in me. There had to be another way.

There was. It involved me relinquishing the big-business swagger with which I had been sauntering around. It involved me surrendering to the idea that this situation would almost certainly pin the failure-tail on my donkey-behind.

The prospect of failure is a funny thing. Especially after all the weeping and gnashing of teeth as we try not to look it in the face. Failure is not Medusa. You don't turn to stone. It's not the end of your quest. In fact, after all the angst and thrashing, there's a freeing release to the idea of potential failure. In particular, when your avoidance of it has been for all the wrong reasons.

Death to . . .

Esther did what she knew she needed to do. Esther released her fear of losing her position and her life. She requested an audience with King Xerxes and told him about Haman's edict.

Esther did the right thing and she didn't die. Yay, Esther! She didn't lose her position as queen, and her obedience resulted in the salvation of the Jews and the death of Haman. Even better. He was hanged and his estate was gifted to Esther, who then appointed Mordecai over it. Now that outcome was entirely suck free!

Like Esther, I also did what I knew I needed to do. I took the original signed contract and put it in a 9x12 envelope and mailed it to the Egyptian company's US office in Hackettstown, New Jersey. I made no photocopies of the document. Once the post office took possession of that envelope, there was no turning back. I had no other proof that the contract existed.

I didn't freak out and I didn't burn up like a supernova. My business survived. The only things that died that day were my fear of failure and the idea that I could litigate my way to business relevance. Like Haman, those things needed to die.

In every spiritual battle, there's a turning point. A moment. A heart choice. A decision that can escalate the conflict or turn the tide completely. Mine was putting all my perceived influence and power in an envelope and sending it to New Jersey. I can say with absolute certainty that I have never regretted that decision. And never will. My Egyptian friends were stunned by my decision and incredibly grateful. Some of my other business associates thought I was a fool. I didn't care. I didn't do it because I thought it was good business.

I did it because I knew it was right.

Epilogue (Such a Funny Word)

A few months ago, I received a phone call from the head of that same Egyptian business group, who wondered if I was open to collaborating on another venture. I declined, but it confirmed in me the path I chose and the man I am today, in part because of that choice.

Esther didn't have the book of Esther to read to help her navigate difficult decision waters. But I did, and I'm forever grateful for the Word of God. Even though the name of God doesn't make an overt appearance in the book of Esther, he was more than obvious to me in every single sentence.

See, I told you it wasn't my main point.

Shun Common

DO WHAT IS RIGHT.
(NOT ADVANTAGEOUS)

Beijing is a gigantic humanity grinder of a city. It's so big and so relentless, I felt even smaller than I normally do in an oversized metropolis. I'd been there before but my schedule had never allowed for too much sightseeing. I'd seen some of the 2008 Olympic stadiums, mostly from the road as we drove past. Saw Tiananmen Square (massive) and the Forbidden City (stoic and imposing).

While fascinating, China is an unusual place to me. Much of its splendor feels heavy. Shrouded in secrecy. It's hard to explain. There is such a fine line between fear and awe. My emotions spent time in both camps when seeing Beijing. People do, and build, some incredible things. Beijing would certainly be near the top of any accomplishment competition.

The most difficult thing for me to explain to you is the Great Wall. The sheer size and scope of the wall made me feel lazy for only writing a book. It was taller and wider than I could have ever imagined. I'm guessing twenty-five feet high and twenty feet wide. I could have comfortably driven a forty-foot motor home on it. With all of its branches, the Great Wall measures out at roughly 13,170 miles in length. The word *great* doesn't do it justice.

And yet, when I stood on and walked the Great Wall, I found myself observing and feeling things I didn't anticipate.

My eyes were drawn to individual tool marks and striations on the massive stones that comprise the wall. Every nick, every angle, every cut, every perfectly formed joint made me wonder about the person who had made them. Was their whole life spent building this wall? Was it a sought-after job or did they dream of a better life? Did they ever wonder what would eventually be on the other side of the wall? Were they married? Could they sing? Were they funny? Did they die here?

Every inch of the Great Wall bears the DNA of backbreaking toil. I sensed these people as I casually strolled on the remains of their lifework.

Don't tell anyone, but it was kind of emotional.

I need to apologize. I might have just wasted ninety seconds of your life. I'll explain why near the end of this chapter.

He's Kind of Like That

All of us have a unique skill set. A fingerprint of the Father on us that, like a snowflake, is one of a kind. We all have strengths that we recognize and use as well as abilities we've yet to discover and mine for their riches.

Me?

One of my greatest strengths is my imagination. I can look at an existing business model and almost always see ways to expand the revenue streams or capitalize on underappreciated strengths within the company. My imagination has always been an asset in the business world. But when it comes to the person of God, it doesn't always serve me well.

The truth is God is so much greater than what I can imagine, conceive, or visualize—though I still imagine, conceive, and visualize away. It's frustratingly necessary for me to attempt to relate to a God that is light-years beyond my ability to fully relate to him. My finite mind remains woefully inadequate for comprehending an infinite God. I don't seek to know him because I expect to successfully bridge that chasm. I do it because I'm commanded to seek him and pursue knowing him.

The word God doesn't do him justice.

On the one hand, I want to grasp who God is and, on the other, I feel a little ashamed at the very idea of thinking I could grasp such a being. I desperately want to know God so I have a starting point for my prayers and conversations with him. On the other hand, I can't imagine having a conversation with the God that flung the stars into existence.

You get me? Like the prophets and songwriters of the Bible, I'm reduced to metaphors and likenesses.

Bonfire at Bill's!

Here's how my imagination process plays out in my life. The Bible says the streets of the New Jerusalem will be paved with gold. It's not really cost effective and wouldn't last long, but we could do that if we wanted. The Bible also says that God sits on a holy throne with Jesus at his right hand. We have thrones here, and to be honest, they're not that neat. I'm not even sure I like the idea that God sits. If I see a chubby cherub playing a harp, I'll most likely push him down! The walls of the New Jerusalem are also reportedly adorned with pearls and all manner of precious stones. Seen 'em! We're told heaven has many mansions. So does Bill Gates's neighborhood. God's presence took the form of a cloud above the tabernacle. Umm, I live in the Seattle area. Enough said. Tents, tablets, robes, bushes, smoke, fire, and white hair? I can see all of that during s'mores night at a nursing home campout. Big whoop.

You see my problem? It's my Great Wall dilemma all over again. Words and visuals fall so far short of the actual thing; it's like trying to find buried treasure by only smelling the back of the treasure map.

I know all these heavenly things will not be as I imagine them. As beautiful as gold is, maybe the gold we see here is just a shadow of what God's perfect gold actually looks like. I'm certain everything in heaven will be way beyond what I could ever imagine or visualize.

I have the same difficulty in trying to reconcile the natural and the supernatural. I can grasp the things that conform to the fixed laws of nature since I can explain or observe them. The supernatural, or miracles, can only be explained by describing the event, not the cause and effect.

I believe in miracles, but for the life of me I couldn't tell you precisely why I do. I've never seen one in person. I'm not talking about a person's cancer disappearing or their chronic pain subsiding. Are these miracles? You bet. But I'm talking about the types of miracles that Jesus performed when he walked the earth. I'm talking about a glass eye rolling across the altar because a new healthy eye popped it out of the socket. I'm talking about a prosthetic arm clattering to the cement as a beautiful new arm suddenly sprouts out of a shoulder. I'm talking about Uncle

Howard sitting bolt upright in his casket and requesting a raspberry scone at his own funeral.

I haven't seen a miracle like this, but I believe in them. I'm not sure why I do. I think the certainty of them is embedded in my innermost being.

Kick-Starting the Convo

If I can picture or imagine God, I've made him way too puny. But if I don't try, he's so foggy I can't conceive of him as my friend. Why did he make me so visual if my visuals distort and undermine, by virtue of their limitations, how magnificent he is? It hurts my head. But not trying to know and imagine him is not possible for me either. I love him.

Words equally fail me, but I can live with that because I've never expected much from them. Lucky you that you picked up my book! At best words kick-start my mind and provide working titles for the whole mess. They're also necessary—inadequate but necessary—for trying to explain my dilemma to you. Is this making sense? Maybe I'm wasting more of your time than I thought.

I reconcile my image problem this way. If I'm going to visualize God or heaven, I'm first and foremost honest with myself. For instance, Jesus was not white. Imagining Jesus as white-skinned starts me out on a false visual foundation and makes it easier to lie to myself about everything else. If I'm going to picture anything about God or his nature, I try to only focus on things that are true. Jesus wasn't strikingly handsome. Imagining him as a great-looking man substitutes things that I find admirable in place of the things he's really about.

But the most effective method I know to relate to God is to clear my mind of all the things I can duplicate or actually imagine and instead focus on his nature alone. I can't accurately define his glory, but he can reveal glimpses of it to my heart. I can't draw a picture of his righteousness, but I can feel the depth of it during my prayers.

My spirit seems to be my only dependable satellite dish for receiving epiphany transmissions from God. My spirit is not hobbled by the same limitations my imagination and vocabulary are.

I could have spent the first fifty pages of this book trying to tell you exactly how it felt to be on the Great Wall of China, and yet I'd never do the experience an ounce of justice. You need to walk your own wall. I could write an infinite number of words and not come close to describing the glory of God. You need to seek him with all that you are. A vicarious experience is never as real or as impacting as an actual one.

I don't believe God would have sacrificed his only Son so he and I could have a casual, arm-punching acquaintance. But his majesty should never be limited by my inability to describe him or held hostage by the cataracts of my mind's eye.

The Great Wall was great. Truly.

But God is so much greater. Truly. Truly.

....   Shun Common   ....

Seek him yourself

Chapter: Relax a Little

Location: Snohomish, Washington

Purpose: Entertaining Foreign Guests

I can't tell you the number of times I have butchered a foreign language. I was always decent at quickly learning the basic greetings and social graces of a country. Hello. Good-bye. Nice to meet you. What's that floating in my soup? Stuff like that. But after a few trips I got bolder and attempted small sentences. No matter how poorly I did, my hosts smiled, nodded, and looked as if they genuinely appreciated the attempt.

They seemed honored that I would try to speak to them in their native tongue, and they never once appeared impatient. This always gave me more confidence than my abilities merited and, I'm sure, led me down the embarrassing-gaff path far more often than I'd ever want to know. There's a good chance what I thought was enthusiasm and appreciation from my foreign friends was actually amusement. Maybe they told Ron jokes once I'd left. Either way, I was memorable!   *true*

But if they'd pointed out my mistakes or continually corrected me, I'm sure I would have shifted my not-so-bilingual lips into park—immediately and for good. It was as if they told me that as long as they could understand the basic concept I was trying to convey, my attempts, no matter how woeful, were more than acceptable. In the moment, I don't think I ever realized the depths of their patience and support. I just thought I was nailing it. In hindsight, what I was doing to their language must have been too gruesome for a Stephen King film.

I have thought about their kindness to me many times, and it's changed me. Fortunately for me, God provided an opportunity for me to return the favor. At least in part.

No Really, Take My Chair

Some years ago, a friend from Japan visited my home. Being an amazingly gracious host, I offered him my leather recliner to sit in as we talked. After a while, he realized what a recliner actually does. It reclines. He tried it quite by accident—with a beverage in his hand.

Whoops.

Once we cleaned up the amber-colored, bubbly spill, he became fascinated with the comfort and function of this uniquely American chair. And some people say the only things the United States excels at today are animated films and Botox injections. I beg to differ. Recliners!

I chalked the experience up as a nice foray into the world of hops-and-barley dry-cleaning adventures. Life and business went on. As part of those business dealings, I regularly sent my friend shipments via ocean freight. It's not uncommon for us to include some small gift with the business items. A couple of weeks before another shipment was to leave the Port of Seattle, my friend emailed me with a request.

He asked if I could include one of those "sofa-for-one, foot-rest, move-back" things. What a great description!

I immediately knew what he wanted: his own recliner. There wasn't a doubt in my mind.

He described it in the only way he knew how. I was not tempted to call him and say, "You silly, unsophisticated Japanese man, you must mean a recliner! Use the right words, please!"

He knew what it looked like. He knew what it felt like to sit in one. He just didn't know what it was called. I was honored to send my friend a recliner, and it didn't matter what he called it. It wouldn't matter to you either. I hope.

Wait for It . . .

So why do we get all mental-bent when we hear even the slightest spiritual misperception from a young Christian? All you relentless Scripture sticklers, I'm giving you the side-eye right now. You know who you are. Pontificate (such a good word!) amongst yourselves. There are times to correct, yes, but there are also times to encourage the spirit of the attempt.

When my son, Riley, was young, he announced that he was "really hoping and praying Satan would stop being so bad and look on the bright side of life." At that particular moment, I found my son's concern for the lost (no matter who it was) far more valuable than correcting him would've been. I wanted to enjoy the moment for the beauty it represented. Going over a detailed travel itinerary for the prince of darkness could wait for another day.

My son's information was incomplete, but his heart was spot-on.

Another time my wife and I were looking for a new church. Our kids were still relatively young. Our daughter was sincere about her faith and had given her heart to the Lord about a year prior. And our son was hand-raisingly enthusiastic about Jesus, to say the very least.

We visited several churches, and the routine was always the same. After the service we'd retrieve our children from Sunday school. The teacher would emerge from the class, beaming from ear to ear with our son in tow like a trout lure.

The teacher would tell us, with barely restrained glee, that our son had accepted Jesus. I don't know how many times he actually accepted Jesus, but it was more than a few.

We usually celebrated with the teacher and let them enjoy their salvation-tally euphoria. Especially if we weren't coming back to that church. After a couple of these conversion experiences, I told our son that he didn't need to keep accepting Jesus and that he was already saved.

He was mature enough to be saved but too green to understand that a weekly affirmation of his salvation wasn't necessary. After I talked to him, he felt as if he had done something wrong and was embarrassed about it.

Why did I do that? What would have been so wrong with my son accepting Jesus every week for another six months? The answer is, "Nothing!" For him, it was a reflection of his enthusiasm for Christ, not a confession of doubt. The way I handled the situation squelched something in him that simply didn't need to be put down. He would have figured it out. Or I could have engaged him by asking questions and showing my mutual enthusiasm for his Christ crush.

No, I don't think he was scarred for life. But my dismissive correction served no long-term benefit to his spiritual maturity. I made it more about me not wanting to see any more of the Cheshire grins from the Sunday school teachers who would track me down and gush about his newly redeemed soul.

As his father, I should have cared more about his love of Jesus than I cared about the inconvenience of feigned joy. Feigning joy was my sin, not his. I should have dashed the teacher's excitement against the rocks long before I ever considered dampening my son's enthusiasm for God.

Teachable Moments Can Have a Fuse

Of course, sometimes we need to correct the misperceptions of a young believer right away. If the thought is contrary to a healthy view of God, nip it in the bud. If it misleads others, set it straight. But other times we need to be more patient and discerning with our input. It won't insult our intelligence to consider the heart of the matter.

Being genuinely thrilled with a "sofa-for-one, foot-rest, move-back" description of how God is revealing himself to the spirit of a new believer can at times be the very best response we can offer.

Let It Ride

My international friends and business associates never made me feel self-conscious about my toddler-like attempts to speak their language. Because of the grace extended to me in other countries, it never crossed my mind to correct and possibly embarrass my Japanese friend for his lack of posterior-perching terminology. So why would I do that to a new follower of Jesus? Correction without a Holy Spirit–led concern for the individual is as useful as barbed-wire dental floss.

Value the person more than your knowledge. Ask yourself if the correction will be encouraging to them or needlessly discouraging to their spirit. If you let it ride, make a mental note and look for a way to add perspective and weight to the truth at a later date. Placing more importance on the heart of a young believer than on our own intellectual egos is affirming for them and a beneficial discipline for us. Two birds with one stone, as it were.

It's okay for us to relax sometimes and enjoy a new believer's process of discovery. There will be lots of time for a fuller understanding of the nuances of God. For now, though, perfectly understandable is perfectly understandable—at any age and in any language.

Shun Common

Chapter: Mommy Dearest

Location: Amsterdam, Netherlands

Purpose: Playing Tourist

I only passed through Amsterdam on my way home from the Middle East, but even so I got a strong sense of the place. Whenever I'm flying into a city for the first time, I like to have a window seat. I want to see the city from the flight path in.

Wow! It was beautiful!

Amsterdam, like every other city, has a feel, a persona. From the air, the area represents itself well. Sprawling fields of flowers and rural farmland surround the airport approach. The city of Amsterdam is also well known for being constructed mostly below sea level. Because of this, the land contains a seemingly endless array of dams, dikes, and levees. The resilience and creative engineering of the people is awe-inspiring.

For quite some time now, Amsterdam has been considered one of the most eco-friendly and environmentally conscious cities in the world. The city is also famous for its claim to contain more bikes than people. I can believe that. You couldn't use a Hula-Hoop there without clunking someone on two wheels.

Most of the people I met were friendly and engaging—except for the young woman at the airport coffee shop. I think I offended her with my casual smile and polite requests. Her countenance was as warm as a drill bit. The tone of her sales presentation was more accusation than information as she not so politely schooled this American on the biodegradable products they used. It felt obvious that, talking to an American, her assumption was that I would naturally be unconcerned about such causes. I considered making her aware that she also was ultimately biodegradable but thought better of it.

What is it about my emotional makeup that tempts me to respond with opposition when someone uses a cause to demean and not to challenge or inspire me? I confess, I feel the same way when I watch Westboro Baptist Church in action. Their antics always compel me not to have compassion for the sin of homosexuality but rather for the person held captive by that sin. Condescension or hate-filled expressions of a belief have always elicited the opposite emotion in me. It's not always a good side of my personality. In the case of Westboro Baptist, my emotional response is spot-on.

In that coffee shop? Not so much. So I swallowed my pride because, ultimately, I shared her concern for the environment.

Still, the environmental passion exhibited in Amsterdam felt a bit . . . off to me. It wasn't exactly over the top. More like incomplete. Not the whole enchilada. What I've never been able to get a handle on is why so many ardent environmentalists are also atheists. Shouldn't Christians hold the eco high ground? This is not a game of "Creator or Creation—you can only have one!" In my experience, though, the lines of division seem to break down that way. It's weird to me.

The Real Language of Programming

I've always believed people are hardwired to understand there is a God. Whenever anthropologists discover a remote, previously unknown tribe, those tribes always have a fundamental understanding of a God or gods. It may be in the form of an albino python or a fossilized prune Danish, but they have them.

People need to be methodically indoctrinated to think and react as if there is no God. Maybe when the earth itself becomes the end-all to your existence, any competing thought is viewed as being adversarial. I don't know for sure. If so, my heart goes out to the people caught up in that either-or mentality.

Maybe Christians themselves are partly to blame for not being front and center on environmental issues. Maybe we think it's an either-or choice between the love of people and the stewardship of God's creation. If so, that's just as sad. And we might well be failing on both fronts.

In Amsterdam many people believe that mother earth is the sole reason for their existence, and they are quite straightforward about that belief. In the United States, we prefer the term "Mother Nature." It feels parental, nurturing, and kind of cuddly. It's not so in-your-face. I get that part. It seems harmless and cute. It's become part of our American vernacular. Meteorologists talk about our weather and natural disasters as the result of Mother Nature's unpredictable influence. It has been so systematically engrained into our consciousness that even Christians use the phrase. I find that strange.

I feel no such inclination.

I don't quite get how a mindless force is a more socially acceptable explanation of our physical world than a deeply involved and personal God.

It's the same in Amsterdam, plus, plus. More sustenance and reverence are associated with old-growth forests than with the eternal God of heaven. Apparently a full-grown tree can nourish some, but it's more difficult to suckle on a stump.

Okay, maybe that was unnecessary. But I've been uncharacteristically complimentary in this chapter so I'm going to leave it in anyway.

Selective Ethics

Some of these energetic earth-first types will spend vast amounts of money to preserve even the most insignificant parcels of wasteland. But the same people will scarcely bat an eye when churches worldwide are burned to the ground and innocent children are slaughtered in the womb for the egregious offense of being conceived at an inconvenient time.

Either-or much?

How does someone get to that place? How seared does a conscience need to be to not see the conscience divide? Is it any wonder that these same people attempt to justify themselves by tirelessly defending the only point of origin they recognize or care about—the earth?

It seems to be a completely natural extension of the mind-set. I have no idea how spiritual cataracts became so fashionable, but I suppose

they will be in vogue until the next horrific tsunami, devastating earth-
quake, or heinous act of violence, terrorism, or genocide.

We seem to find God convenient and acceptable at those times.

Save the What?

Like me, the people of Amsterdam are seeking purpose. The need for
purpose is insatiable in all of us. But purpose is a funny thing. It can't
be plucked out of thin air.

If not interpreted through a foundational premise, purpose ceases
to be a definable or justifiable pursuit. Like it or not, I can't choose both
the god of nature and the nature of God. This is the only real either-or.

Unfortunately, once the obvious answer of God has been kicked to the
curb, creation provides the only available alternative to satisfy that need
for purpose. Seldom will the same people consider where their desire for
purpose comes from in the first place. They satisfy themselves with the
banality of feel-good causes. They exalt themselves as defenders of the
inanimate and the morally neutral, the benevolent kings and queens of
all things dirt. Like Vladimir Lenin's "useful idiots" they parade their
pampered personas in front of the lights and cameras and utter phrases
like "Save the planet!"

Just an observation here: If God didn't exist and Earth was all there
was for us, it would scarcely require us to save it. Planet Earth would be
just fine, with or without us. If humans polluted and pillaged the earth
to the point of it being uninhabitable *for us*, the earth would continue to
rotate and orbit the sun.

The earth does not cry out to be saved. Some are genuinely concerned
about the condition of the planet. I think that's true. But I have little
doubt that what some of them are really saying is, "Save us! Save me!"

Funny, isn't it? Even in our denial of God and the exaltation of nature,
most people are still keenly aware of their need to be saved.

A Natural Conclusion

Is God a tree, a flower, a whale, a mountain, a smile, a cloud, a river,
or a tapeworm? No. But these things quietly attest to his remarkably

creative hand and his love of beauty. To our spiritual eyes and ears, all things created, although individually quiet, corporately form a symphony of finely tuned praise and worship–filled symmetry to the One who spoke them into existence.

Nature merely confirms that which is intrinsically known and seems so obvious to me as to be unmovable. The cosmological, teleological, ontological, and moral arguments for the existence of God are, in my mind, conclusive.

The Devour Hour

When looked at cleanly, the creation resoundingly confirms God's existence and character and stands in stark contrast to the purposeless, impersonal, random nature we ascribe to it.

I've learned not to shrink back in places like Amsterdam. Logic and desire are on my side. I've learned that my understanding of the natural world is sufficient to engage those with whom I come in contact.

At the end of the day, Darwinists are seeking truth, just like me. The difference is that mine is an individual conclusion, a relationship. Theirs is a form of intellectual fish-schooling that dissuades any deeper discussion of competing or perceived supernatural alternatives. They dart around in unison and provide the Devourer an easy and satisfying target.

I don't feel intellectually inferior for recognizing the divine. I refuse to cower to fiction dolled up as logic.

My Sin

Here's what really shames me. I'm a weird breed. I need to call it like it is. My natural inclination to oppose a movement just because I don't like the spiritual implications associated with it is sin. It is. My either-or attitude is no more admirable than theirs. I don't need to subscribe to their entire manifesto in order to do the right thing. As a Christian I should be a vigilant environmentalist.

There, I said it. I feel better. Let's hug.

Not because I see the earth as a point of origin, but because of God's sovereign will that spoke it into existence and his hand that sustains it. I need to stop trying to make my point by thumbing my nose at those who use the same activity for their own edification. I can't make my point by ignoring my responsibility. The earth is not worthy of my worship but, given the hand that made it, it is ultimately worthy of my stewardship and responsible care.

Use It or Lose It

I don't ever want to lose the love and beauty of what I saw in Amsterdam, in the people, the geography, and the culture. I want the opportunity to know and call these people friends. One day I want to go back to the Netherlands and engage more fully with them. Even if they initially think of me as a wasteful and ambivalent American. I can deal with that. Challenge accepted!

Opportunity often masquerades as ridicule. The truth is, I will miss the people of Amsterdam because I know Jesus misses them more. (Deep sigh.)

Yes, even the coffee shop princess.

Last thought. I find it telling that the acronym for mother earth just so happens to be ME. Interesting, don't you think?

.... Shun Common ....

In almost every country I've opened coffee shops, finding and securing a "can't-miss" location is not even close to a predictable science—especially if you don't have a recognizable brand.

Opening a smaller chain of retail shops of any kind is a dicey proposition, especially in a country like Egypt and a district like Heliopolis. Heliopolis is a bubbling bowl of ethnic stew. It's one of only a few districts in Cairo that is comprised of a great many foreigners. Because of this demographic mix, you will find all the typical American fast-food joints. Sad but true. Name-brand recognition is more important here than other places in Egypt because of the market. Even the evil empire of the coffee world (yes, you know who I'm talking about) has had their fair share of missteps and failures in this part of Egypt.

Still, I wanted to try my hand at opening a coffee shop in Heliopolis. I knew it was risky. There are so many complex factors that go into a successful coffee shop that every one of them feels like a combination of due diligence, demographics, vision, discipline, community relevance, and blind-stinking luck.

I've seen mediocre locations succeed and amazing locations fail miserably. An amazing location has it all: high visibility, easy access, ample exterior signage, adequate parking, great foot and drive-by traffic, a high per capita income, a good mix of residential and retail, low crime, some form of mass transit nearby, and a favorable lease rate. A mediocre location might have six or seven of those ten attributes. Sometimes the reason for a location's failure is obvious, and sometimes it's a complete mystery. When they do fail, it's important, if possible, to figure out why.

It's also a really uncomfortable process.

Once a shop fails, everyone just wants to wash their hands of it and move on. Nobody likes failing in such a public arena. No one enjoys sifting through the smoldering embers after a four-alarm business inferno. And I've had to dance and sniff around the flames my fair share of times.

No matter the level of experience or key indicators I applied, I still felt like I was trying to cut my own hair in the dark.

That Church Is on Fire

I've experienced the same head-scratching conundrums in the churches my family and I have been around. I don't know what percentage of church plants survive the first three years, but I'm willing to bet it's hanging out in the under-30-percent club. Cracking the church-planting code seems as risky as hanging a business shingle. The process gets even dicier if you're not a big-box church brand.

I've seen churches with what seemed like can't-miss locations die a slow and painful death. I've seen churches with mature, vibrant congregations and theologically sound leaders dwindle and fold up like an origami trout. Other churches remain but lose their spiritual DNA and slowly morph into a creature no one recognizes. Still others go up in metaphorical flames and turn into disbanded, Jesus-follower dust overnight.

What's up with that? Were they just shekel-fueled holograms of community relevance? Did they start out as ordained by God only to lose their way? Or were they manufactured expressions of obedience to begin with? Like my coffee-shop conundrum, it's a head scratcher to be sure.

I'm far from an authority on why churches fail, but (as you might have guessed) I'd like to suggest what I think is one of the major soul-sucking culprits in any church demise.

Bored with Boards

Do you remember the pin screen fad that swept the nation in the mid eighties? If you don't, humor me as I try to describe it. Or take a moment and Google it. I'll wait.

They were marketed under several brand names (Pin Art Board, Pinscreen, PinPressions, and Pinhead). I'll just call it a pin screen. They were made from a medium-sized, rectangular piece of perforated pressboard (usually painted black), a sheet of clear Plexiglas of the same size, spacers, and hundreds of large, blunt, straight pins. The pressboard and Plexiglas formed a sandwich with an inch and a half of space between them. The pins went freely through the pressboard with the pinheads inside and facing the Plexiglas. All the narrower pin ends stuck out the back of the pressboard when tipped down. If you pressed your hand in the back ends of the pins, a three-dimensional likeness of your hand would emerge on the other side in the pinheads.

We good so far?

They were fun to goof around with for the better part of three minutes before they became tiresome. There were only so many things people wanted to see a chrome likeness of and even fewer things one wanted to push into a bunch of straight pins.

But it was always fun to close your eyes, gently press your face into the pins, and voilà! A gleaming chrome likeness of your face would emerge on the other side.

Now imagine the pin screen represents a church—any church, every church—and every pin represents a member of that congregation. Still with me? Good. Now imagine Jesus strolls up to our pin-screen church and confidently presses his face against the back of the pins. As we look on, his likeness emerges on the other side. The depiction is so shiny and perfect that everyone immediately recognizes the face of Christ. Jesus then smiles, gives his new pin-screen church a "make me proud" fist pump, and vanishes into plump air. (The air's older now. It happens.)

Chrome on the Throne

The church hits the street with its new, gleaming visage of Jesus. People are saved and lives are transformed by the accuracy of his likeness. But as time goes by, a few members stop operating in their God-given gifts, step back, and just go through the motions. Their individual pins fall to the back of the board.

Politics and egos bring about rifts in the church that marginalize a group of members—and a few more pins fall away. Pervasive gossip causes some members to be distrustful of others—and their pins fall away. As those who are new in Christ watch mature Christians disengage, they follow suit—and more pins fall to the back. If the Bible ceases to be taught as God intended, people lose strength and vision from a lack of foundational truths—and even more pins disappear.

At some point, enough pin-people fall away or relinquish their ordained purpose in the church body that the face of Christ becomes a little difficult to identify. If more pin-people slip to the back of the board, the face of Christ becomes severely obscured. And finally, when too many pin-people retract, the face of Christ is completely unrecognizable to the community the church was meant to serve.

Once the likeness of Jesus cannot be clearly identified, that church becomes as effective as a gold-plated aspirin. It might be shiny and pretty, but it won't put a dent in the community's headaches any longer.

Pin Pals

If the only seriously engaged members of a church are the staff and a small percentage of the congregation, they better hope the land the church sits on turns out to be a platinum mine, otherwise the church will cease to be of any real value. Nothing is quite as sad as a once smoking-hot church slowly assuming tomb temperature.

If I don't want to be a contributing factor in the decomposition of my church's portrayal of Jesus, I need to serve. Truthfully, if my only intent was to coast and gossip, I'd be more beneficial to the body of Christ if I just slept in on Sundays. My fervent pursuit of disengaged nothing is not of actual benefit to anyone.

We all must recognize and respond to our role within a specific church body as well as the greater body of Christ. The same holds true for my coffee shops. I can rely on formulas, traffic studies, and boxed solutions, or I can engage in the process. Train employees, pull some espresso shots, talk to the customers, warm up a scone, interact with the community, and generally be in the mix.

Workers in some countries don't feel comfortable with the president of the corporation rolling up their sleeves and getting a little dirty. I've had to buck that trend on more than one occasion. It's important for me and gives me a level of understanding I couldn't get in any other way. I can see what the deficits are and make changes to the business model for that particular shop. I can expand or contract services if they are beneficial or not well received. Having my shoes behind the counter and talking to the customers provides a level of information that I could not acquire anywhere else or in any other way.

Rolling Around in the Mud *Is* the Clean Up

The same principle holds true for our involvement in our church. I'm a very real part of the face of Christ in my church and in my community. Yes, even when I don't feel like it or choose not to walk it out.

Nobody should be above service. No matter their position or title. There are things I can't learn about the people in my community or my Christian compadres in any other way. Without me or you, the likeness of Jesus loses just a little of its clarity to the people who most need to recognize it.

We are more valuable to God's purposes in our church than we may realize. Nobody else but you and I can fill the roles we were designed for in the specific church God has for us. Once we know that, we can't unknow it. We can only choose to ignore it.

Don't do that.

If your church fails, roll around in that soot and mud for a while until you've learned a little something about your own culpability in the demise. If our church is not as dynamic or as Christlike as we'd hoped, the issue might not be our church. It might be our lack of engagement in it. Our view becomes drastically different when we're mixing it up and serving, shoulder to shoulder, with the other employees—or saints.

Yes, I know. Technically I just called myself a pinhead, but if I'm engaged and serving with love, at least I'm a really useful one!

Chapter: Fear Knot

Location: Bogotá, Colombia

Purpose: Preliminary Meeting

Bogotá, Colombia, is an interesting place.

I'm being kind.

It's big and sort of dirty. And although it's not as dangerous as some other countries I've visited, it obviously has its moments.

Today was one of those moments. My host drove me to a mall to have lunch. The mall had an underground parking lot. As we pulled up to the pay station to enter the garage, I saw armed guards. This is not uncommon in many countries. Security personnel are routinely positioned in public places, hotels, and tourist attractions. No big deal.

What I didn't expect was to have them check the trunk for guns and use mirrors to search under the car for bombs. Bombs and guns? Where was I? This was supposed to be the rich-soiled, benevolent land of milk and coffee. What happened to that kind, hardworking, harmless man, Juan Valdez, and his coffee bean–laden burro? Juan's loving portrayal of a typical Colombian coffee farmer still holds a special place in my heart. Yes, I know he's a fictional character from a long-running ad campaign— but it was a really good campaign!

Beyond Senor Valdez, I don't know what I expected from Bogotá, but I wasn't prepared to be on pants-peeing high alert. I can usually predict the countries I need to be cautious in based on the State Department's travel site. I hadn't even checked before flying to Colombia. The really dangerous drug cartels were in Cali and Medellin, not Bogotá.

That night in my hotel room I watched the news. The telecast was filled with stories of murders, violence, drug wars, political unrest, and corruption. Sure enough, Bogotá was no garden spot of tranquility.

Duly noted. I kind of knew now it would be a rough place, not to mention the bombs-and-weapons search at the mall that still unnerved me.

As I lay in bed, in the pitch black of my hotel room, my imagination got the better of me. What is it about being alone in another country that makes circumstances seem more threatening and the darkness feel more ominous?

I started going over my activities from the day. Was I followed? Did anyone seem to be watching me? Were they planning to kidnap me and hold me in the jungle until they got what they wanted? I had no idea what my trade value was anymore. I hoped it wasn't embarrassingly low. I hoped I didn't have to find out. But it was likely more than I could work off as a farmhand at a coca plantation.

The anxiety formed a knot in the pit of my stomach. I started hearing unusual noises. It was dark—so very dark. I couldn't find perspective like I could during the day. And the suffocating darkness in that room dragged me all the way back to my childhood fears.

Trolling for Hope

There was a time growing up when I feared the dark. Although I can't replicate the actual childlike fear of the dark, the anxiety I felt back then is easily accessed.

Lying in my dark hotel room felt the same.

Like me, most children pass through this phase relatively unscathed. The dark ceases to be the brooding, insidious troll I used to imagine it. But that night, Colombia dredged it up in me.

Nighttime can make my problems and fears seem far more insurmountable than they appear in the light of day. But at that moment, my fear wasn't completely irrational. It had an element of reality associated with it. Still, I needed to get my imagination in check, so I did what I always do.

I talked to God about it.

His response came to me by way of a calm assurance that he was more than comfortable with darkness.

But God *is* light. How could this be?

Here's what he whispered to me in the darkness of that Bogotá hotel room.

Darkness. It's a word, to be sure. But what is darkness anyway? The truth is darkness is nothing. Zippo.

Light is something. It's quantifiable. It can be observed and measured. We may not know if light is a wave or a particle or a combination of both, but we know it's something.

Darkness is merely the absence of light. Total darkness is the absence of all light.

I know he's comfortable there, but I wonder if God actually likes the dark. It probably doesn't matter. Light, dark—maybe it's all the same to him. So why do I consider dark to be so threatening and scary?

Why do you?

Coffins and Light Sabers

I think Dracula strikes a particular chord of fear in those who read the book or see one of the numerous movies, not because Dracula is invincible but because he is only active during the time when his victims are at rest.

The idea of being asleep, unaware, and defenseless against an attacker is a fear that goes to the very heart of my sense of security. During the night, I feel more vulnerable. During the day I'd stand a reasonable chance of subduing the cape-clad lad and getting him to a competent oral surgeon.

I doubt Darth Vader's breathing would seem as ominous if he weren't fully dressed in a black cloak and mask, his face obscured. (I wonder how he brushed his teeth or used lip balm.) I think if I saw big Darth dressed in a pastel version of his outfit, cape flowing and unmasked, I might be more inclined to suggest an effective decongestant or bronchial inhaler than I would to fear him.

Playing on Our Fears

Is darkness really as I imagine it to be? While I concede that the Bible speaks of darkness as an attribute of evil, I do not concur that the actual atmosphere of darkness is a place where only evil resides and operates.

I wanted to get on top of this fear, so I started to highlight some of the really incredible things that have come to me by way of the darkest routes.

For instance, God brought forth his creation out of complete darkness. The first couple of verses in the Bible read, "In the beginning God created the heavens and the earth. Now the earth was formless and empty, darkness was over the surface of the deep, and the Spirit of God was hovering over the waters." Prior to that his Spirit was present in the darkness, but it was still really dark.

Jesus was miraculously conceived in the total darkness of Mary's womb. That was a good moment too. You once resided in the darkness of your own mother's womb and were completely without fear.

Jesus Christ rose from the dead in the utter blackness of a tomb, tucked away from the prying eyes of those bent on his permanent demise. Also a good thing.

God has made us subject to the renewing and refreshing cycle of rest. Sleep for most everyone takes place in the dark, and even if it's not dark outside, we try to replicate the dark to sleep more restfully.

In the deepest and darkest depths of the world's oceans, life flourishes. It is only in darkness that we can see with the naked eye a tiny sliver of the remarkable cosmic expanse of God's universe. Fireworks would be pretty boring without the backdrop of night.

The process of salvation is the result of an unmistakable but completely unseen transformation in the darkest depths of our being. The Bible and life are replete with examples of the glorious things that have happened and still take place today in the unseen places of darkness.

I think I've been too harsh to the dark. Yes, God is light and we are called to be lights in the world, but without darkness, light loses its effect. It just does.

My point is that darkness is not the exclusive domain of the unholy or dangerous. God has wrought some of his more miraculous feats in dark and unseen places. As a child, I wish that someone had told me all the incredible things God has done for me in the dark. I might have still been afraid of the dark, but it would not have seemed nearly as terrifying.

At least he told me that night in Bogotá. In the darkness of my hotel room, in a beautiful but marginally dangerous country, seeing darkness for what it is helped.

Okay, Logic, You Win Tonight

I hope I can learn to appreciate darkness a little more and fear it a little less, especially when I'm alone and far away from home. I'm starting to think darkness has an unjustified reputation. A bad rap. I should have waited for the daylight before I was too hard on the dark. And anyway, I'm pretty sure I had more pressing issues to worry about in Colombia than nighttime. The very worst things for me take place in the darkness of my own unrepentant heart, not in a Bogotá hotel room. Those are the real circumstances I should be on high alert for.

Okay, Bogotá, let's start over. I judged you too harshly. I should have calmed down, slept, then gotten up the next morning and given you a mulligan. Your darkness was no worse than mine.

We good?

.... *Shun Common* ....

Chapter: My Life as an Altar Boy

Location: Tokyo, Japan

Purpose: Opening a Coffee Shop

I've had a number of fist-pumping, adrenaline-filled, I-have-to-tell-somebody-(in-English) successes in my business life. They were exhilarating, to say the least. Most of those moments happened in other countries, so the majority of my celebrating took place over a five-dollar can of soda and a four-dollar bag of potato chips from the minibar in my room.

Oh yeah, I pulled out all the stops.

Conversely, I've had a number of humiliating failures that, at the time, seemed to suck every ounce of wind from my sails.

Where am I going with this? If I told you now, it wouldn't be a surprise! I like surprises.

Amped and Cramped

One specific failure refuses to stop playing on the movie screen in my mind. It was early in my business ventures and my Japanese partner had secured a location that was only a block from the Yaesu Central exit at Tokyo Station.

I flew over to Japan to open a coffee shop at that location. My partner and I were going to personally open up, work, train, and oversee for the first two weeks of the grand opening. I was amped up and ready to pull some espresso shots and prove how bad my conversational Japanese was.

Money was scarce in those early days, so the plan was only feasible if I stayed at a really cheap hotel. Hotels anywhere near the location were anything but cheap. So, accommodations had been made for me at a hotel in the blue-collar suburb of Nishi-Nippori. I thought, *Hey, it's on* the *Yamanote Line and, although it's quite a jaunt from the main part of town, I won't even have to transfer trains.* The price per night was better than I imagined, and according to the map on the train station wall, it was only about seven stations away.

The map was clearly not to scale.

And lest I forget, this shop opening was taking place in the dead of winter.

PEZ Dispensers

The night before the opening, I boarded the train and made my way to my hotel. It would be good to settle in, read a book, and get some rest before the craziness of the opening ensued.

As I watched out the train window, the surroundings got bleaker and bleaker. Skyscrapers gave way to shorter, rusted manufacturing buildings, and those eventually gave way to a part of Tokyo I had no idea existed. The only things gleaming there were the oil slicks on the water and ice-filled potholes.

I found my way to the hotel. The lobby was as inviting as a Siberian gulag. Yikes! Not a single person in the entire hotel spoke a word of English. I was viewed with impassive contempt by the staff. These were not the warm, inviting, and wonderful Japanese people I had come to know!

Then I got to the phone booth they called a room. Except for eighteen inches from the end of the bed to the wall, the bed took up every bit of space in the room. The bathroom (and I only call it a bathroom because of the recognizable fixtures) was lovingly and carefully constructed to accommodate an individual the size of Yoda. I'm six feet tall and weigh about 190 pounds. Okay, 195. My head, torso, and one butt cheek could fit comfortably in the space.

No matter. I would make the best of it. I was there to open a coffee shop right by one of the busiest train stations in the world. It was an important business milestone for me. That was my focus. Not my cubically frugal room. I could do this.

My schedule for the next two weeks straight went like this: I received a wake-up call at three forty-five. I showered, dressed, and made my way through the bone-chilling wind and snow to the train station five blocks away. I rode the train for forty minutes to Tokyo Station, got off the train, and walked to the coffee shop. Being in the city didn't help the brr factor.

My partner and I did the preopening procedures and then opened the shop at five thirty. I worked all day and closed the location down at seven thirty. Closing procedures took a little more than an hour. I would have a bite to eat and board the train back to my lovely and spacious rent-a-tin-shack. I would usually enter my room around ten thirty and do my best to be in bed by eleven.

For two weeks!

Near the end of the two weeks, I was so exhausted I think I actually fell asleep on the jarring, cramped train ride. Head back, mouth gaping. You know the look. I must have resembled a PEZ dispenser. I didn't care.

 I was still young and primarily propelled by glands and caffeine, so the schedule, though brutal, was doable. I don't know what made this particular two-week span one of the longest of my life. But it was. It might have been the combination of the schedule, the stifling accommodations, the bleak surroundings, the frigid cold, and the loneliness of not knowing a soul or understanding almost anything that was being said to me or about me that made it so daunting. Whatever it was, by the end of those two weeks, I wasn't sure I even liked the coffee industry anymore.

But I had survived it. It was done. I had never been so happy to get back home and whine to my wife. Lucky her.

The shop remained open for about a year. Then, for a number of reasons, it wasn't economically sustainable and we had to shut it down. The most difficult shop opening of my life had ended in a very public failure. Talk about insult to injury.

I wanted to erase that experience from my business story. I needed to. How could it possibly be anything more than a squandered portion of my life I couldn't get back? What a waste.

Or so I thought at the time.

I Fail, to See the Light

I used to believe the euphoric, victorious Jesus moments were the times that God used to sustain me. I liked telling those parts of my business story.

I'm not so sure about that anymore. For me, the problem is not the need for those undeniable God events to sustain me, but the ones I consider to be important. In the midst of an emotionally dry season or a time of heart-wrenching struggle, what are those things that keep us all spiritually sane?

For me, shop failure and all, it's times like those two weeks in Nishi-Nippori. Let me tell you why.

The Cost of Cost

The Bible recounts many instances where the Israelites built altars to mark a spot where God exhibited his faithfulness to them. I started to think about the altar-building moments in my life. Where had God shown up for me, as surely as rust and boogers? (Some things take longer to form than others.)

Without exception, my personal altars to the Lord either will remain vibrant and impacting or, as time passes, they will dissolve into faded and tattered versions of themselves. If I want them to endure, I need to choose my altar locations wisely, like King David did.

This Might Hurt a Little

In 2 Samuel 24, King David, in response to his own prideful disobedience and a prophet's instruction, went to build an altar to the Lord on the site of a traumatic plague. Seventy thousand people had died in a national tragedy, and this spot David went to was like Israel's ground zero. This was the place. No other site would carry the emotional weight that this one would.

David approached the owner of this land and asked to purchase the area. The owner of the property, Araunah, said he would give it willingly to David. David, however, insisted on paying for it. He told Araunah he would not build an altar and sacrifice offerings to the Lord that cost him nothing. David understood that for the altar and the subsequent offering to have real bandwidth, they needed to cost him something.

Does that mean that God cannot stir me to change through a sweet time of worship or prayer? Of course he can. Great successes? Love 'em. But if the event really stings, I remember it. If I've sacrificed something I hold dear, it sticks to me like pine pitch.

I remember joy, but my being is transformed by sacrifice and suffering.

Houston, We Have a Problem

A number of years back, I went through an ordeal that rattled me to my very core. I'm not exaggerating. Had I not built my God altars on circumstances that endured, I'm not sure I would have found my way back fully, or at least not as quickly.

By business association, I was drawn into a federal lawsuit based entirely on the actions of others. I'll own up to my mistakes. Most won't. They didn't. But I felt clean in this instance.

It didn't matter.

The financial requirements to defend yourself in such a proceeding can be off the charts. And they were. The lawsuit lasted more than two years. If I were a criminal, free legal counsel would've been provided to me.

I wasn't. When the smoke cleared, I had been drained of absolutely everything I ever worked for. The reasons why are not the story here. The reality was, I was starting over at a time when I thought I was just hitting my business stride. In an instant, I was flat broke—actually massively in debt—and I had no solid idea of how to change any of it.

I was like the men on Apollo 13 when they had to do a final fuel burn to correct their course. They only had enough fuel for one shot at it. It had to be perfect. If they entered the earth's atmosphere too steeply, they would become a charcoal briquette. If they came in too shallow, they would skip off the atmosphere and be jettisoned into outer space.

The reentry into my own faith walk felt just as precarious. I felt like I only had enough resilience-fuel for one shot at it. I needed to rely on my own life altars to guide the angle of my reentry and bring me fully back to a place of safety and service.

Those two weeks in Tokyo, in the dead of winter, in a microscopic hotel room, with an exhausting schedule, came flooding back to me.

If I could do that, I could do this.

I felt like I could draw from that time as if it had happened only the day before. It was as potent and as reliable as it had ever been. For me, that altar was my ground zero in the restoration of my faith and finances.

A Laundry List

Have you ever washed and then dried a load of jeans? Random? Why, yes, it is. If you're like me, I clean the lint trap as soon as the load of clothes is dry. Ever notice that after drying your jeans all the lint is blue? That's because the stuff in there is not some free floating lint that just happens to end up on your pants. The stuff that's in there used to be part of your pants. Your jeans are slowly deteriorating.

During the lifelong reclamation of my calamity-prone heinie, my moments of business euphoria have deteriorated in me like my blue jeans in the lint trap of life. They don't seem to time-travel well.

But sacrifice, that which was brutally tough for me, maintains its intensity in me and endures like a conspiracy theory.

My time during that shop opening was one of the most difficult but empowering events in my life. I realized that I could do almost anything for a season and that there was life and real value in my greatest failures. The most resilient and impacting events in my life have been the ones that emotionally or physically cost me dearly. I have learned and drawn from that time more than any single moment of success.

I don't know. I might be a bit odd or it might just be the coffee talking, but I kind of dig failure. There's substance in it. It's beefy.

I thought landing the location next to Tokyo Station was the important altar. Nope. My most bulletproof altar was located on the corner of Failure Avenue and Sacrifice Drive. That spot was the real-life prize.

Surprise!

Shun Common

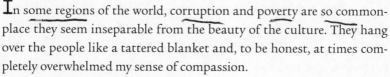

Chapter: Coffee Amigos

Location: Tegucigalpa, Honduras

Purpose: Negotiating a Licensing Deal

In some regions of the world, corruption and poverty are so commonplace they seem inseparable from the beauty of the culture. They hang over the people like a tattered blanket and, to be honest, at times completely overwhelmed my sense of compassion.

This was one of those places.

It seemed like everyone had an angle. It felt like everyone I came in contact with wanted something from this pasty American. I was a patsy—a pasty patsy. To the locals, I seemed to be little more than privileged guilt in a suit.

It was a weird sensation. Most other times I accepted it and remained joyful. But on this trip I couldn't muster a genuine smile to save my life. Any possibility of forging a new friendship seemed unlikely and, truth be told, ill-advised. My spidey sense was so overloaded I couldn't tell who genuinely wanted to get to know me and who was merely trolling for information to exploit an emotional angle.

So I punted. I closed up, shut down, and stayed guarded. Compassion? Not this trip. I was too leery to access that part of my heart. I was the Fort Knox of businessmen.

In the Zone

I was staying at a beautiful hotel I'd stayed at a number of times over the years, right in the heart of Tegucigalpa. I could relax in that hotel. It was, by Central American standards, swanky. The marble, the pool, the palm trees, the staff, everything about the place was comfortable and set me at ease. It was my air-conditioned fortress of safety and predictability. The only thing people wanted from me there were tips—and I could deal with that.

Directly across the street from my hotel was a mall that rivaled the average American counterpart. The entrance to the mall was a cauldron of activity: taxi drivers seeking fares, cars honking, people scurrying about, and street kids roaming the sidewalks panhandling. So many kids! Didn't anyone here go to school?

Each morning before my meetings, I'd enjoy a latte at the coffee shop in the mall. This was my out-of-fortress autopilot time. I followed the international "bug off, buddy" rules to a tee: blank stare, purposeful stride, an air of ambivalent importance. I was locked in. I would not be scammed, bothered, or trifled with!

Mauled at the Mall

But as I left my hotel and crossed the street to the mall on a late April morning, two young street boys spotted me and somehow made eye contact.

Impressive. The game was afoot.

I casually angled away from a direct path to the mall entrance, hoping to confuse them. I nodded, smiled, and made eye contact with other people so they might think I was a local businessman. My tactical behavior remained flawless.

It didn't help. They were that good.

Their "rich American" radar pinged like hail on trash can lids. They were locked on. Now desperate, I panicked. I faked left and bolted right, but it was too late. They had outflanked me, outmaneuvered me, and outsmarted me, and all three of us knew it. Pint-sized street ninjas to be sure. I considered retreating to the hotel to regroup and wait them out. The traffic was too bad for that. I would have to deal with them. I was a grown man and they were just kids, for goodness' sake!

But as I looked down at them, I didn't see kids; I saw only inconvenience and bottomless need. I felt no compassion. Resigned to my guilt-assuaging fate, I reached into my pocket to find a suitable dead-president offering.

As my hand emerged, I saw a twenty-dollar bill in my hand.

Wrong pocket!

I have a panhandler pocket of small bills and local currency for such emergencies. Again, too late. Their eyes looked like four beaming beach balls. If it were possible for a human being to crack their face from smiling too hard, these boys would have required some serious mug spackling.

I knelt down and, in the worst Spanish ever spoken, said that it was to be divided evenly between them. They nodded, smiled, grabbed the bill, and ran up the street at a dead sprint.

The taxi drivers and locals stared at me like I was a gigantic lollipop. I've looked dumb before. I was good at it. No big deal. I shrugged off the embarrassment of being outwitted by a couple of nine-year-olds and continued to the coffee shop.

I was sure that was that.

A Pesky Little Fellow

The next morning as I left the hotel, I looked up. One of the boys stood on the other side of the street in his brand-new jeans and tennis shoes. Same beaming grin as the day before. Ear to ear.

He said nothing when I reached the other side of the street and merely walked beside me as I made my way to the mall coffee shop. I ordered my usual latte and ordered him a blended fruit drink. The little gremlin couldn't afford to have his growth stunted by coffee. We sat in silence and enjoyed our drinks together. The smile never left his face. When we were done, he walked beside me until I went back inside the hotel. He waved and left.

Every morning he'd come alongside me as I went to the coffee shop and peel off when I went back to my hotel. He never asked me for more money. He never spoke and he never stopped smiling.

On the final day of my trip, I told him I was leaving the next morning. He smiled and nodded, and then his face grew serious. He pointed to me and then at himself and asked a one-word question.

"Friends?"

I surrendered. Completely. I broke inside. All my uppity, manicured emotions came crashing in on my heart. A boy, a persistent little kid, had broken my professional persona with one word.

At that moment, I didn't care who saw me or what anyone might think. The sounds around us hushed and the bustle blurred. I knelt, looked at him, nodded, and said, "Yes, we're friends." And I meant it!

The look on his face was one of utter relief and satisfaction. A contentedness washed over him as he straightened his posture. With that, he smiled, turned, and walked away.

I have never seen him since.

Big Lesson, Small Teacher

I thought I was on a really important business trip to Tegucigalpa, Honduras.

Nope.

As it turned out, I was there to befriend a remarkable boy—a child of the streets. The importance of my friendship to him still snuffs out my pesky penchant for apathy. To this very day I see children differently than I did before I met my young Honduran friend. Before him, I really only felt emotionally invested in the lives of my own children. But that waist-high sidecar of a kid altered my insides permanently. In the end, he only wanted to be known and considered as valuable to me. He was. And as far as other kids go, they were now as well.

With nothing more than silence and smiles, a young Honduran boy taught me how to see people, not just look at them. He taught me how to recognize the glimmer of the divine through the haze of language, culture, poverty, and age. In that moment, I saw him as a child, a young man, an adult, a husband, and a father. He looked innocent and formidable at the same time. There was a life, a fire, a something in his eyes that made me marvel. No more than you can see in the eyes of most children, I suspect. I had just gotten comfortable looking past the future.

Not that day.

That day, I really saw *him*, and it changed *me*. To this day, I'm glad the little barnacle attached himself to me as firmly as he did.

I even found myself looking for him at the airport as I waited to board my flight home. I miss that kid. I miss being outmaneuvered by him on the streets. I miss his ridiculously large smile. His joy owns a piece of my heart. I can't recall what the other little boy even looked like. I only remember the huge smile and lively eyes of my friend. I never even knew his name but his impact on my life stays with me. I also choose to keep that experience altar in good condition. It's important to me.

Sometimes I wonder if he ever thinks of me. I hope he still draws from our time together and keeps it safely tucked away in his heart. I still consider myself his friend, and him mine. One day, on the other side of frailty, I hope to thank him for his life-changing friendship . . . and the vision correction.

Shun Common

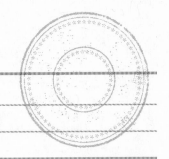

Chapter: Rock the Giant
Location: Multiple Countries
Purpose: Coffee-Related Muck

The international business world can be intoxicating. Extremely. The intrigue of travel, the unfamiliar but fascinating customs and sights, and the strange food and languages are an irresistible lure. For a person wired like me, it's a veritable feast for my adventure senses.

And if I'm completely honest, I always get a sense of freedom from the lack of personal historical context. Most of the people I've met or known in other countries only knew me as I was then, present day. They had no clue who I was growing up or in my early years of business. They hadn't witnessed the litany of suspect choices I'd made in my past. I could be the today me, not a battered remnant of my past.

I could also be the dynamic Christian I always wanted to be. A man full of grace and mercy. A leader by example and a servant by choice. An ambassador for my native land and my eventual home in heaven. Nobody knew otherwise. For this guy, it was a big ole lungful of sweet freedom. Overseas, my life felt like a beer commercial. Happy people with no problems, enjoying sandy, tropical beaches and sipping suds with other smiling, pretty people.

Yes, I know I'm no model. That's why I said it "felt" like a beer commercial. (Plus I'm not a big beer drinker.)

In other countries, my Christian walk was like the perfect balance of acceptance hops and clean-slate barley. Refreshing and delicious. Oh, *I* knew it wasn't true. I still had my bouts with doubt. But my business colleagues didn't, and that type of unfamiliarity was, well, Snoopy-dance worthy. I reveled in it. I savored it.

Here's why.

Dirt-Bag Brand

Much of my childhood was an unmitigated disaster. (I love the word "unmitigated" even though I can't say it without sounding British.) And there's no question my teen years and early twenties were a train wreck. Ever since, a number of people, family and otherwise, have always felt more comfortable relating to me based on who I was during those two chunks of my youth rather than who I am now.

I was a liar. And a thief. It's true. I didn't win the senior superlative for "most likely to be incarcerated," but not much more was expected of me. Understandable. What I lacked in discipline I made up for with a wealth of irresponsibility. (That is called *sarcasm*, by the way.) I was a keeper!

For a number of years, I didn't fight the identity. I thought it was better to be mocked than completely ignored. But God changed my heart and the lights slowly went on.

It didn't matter.

For many of the people closest to me, it was easier to relate to me based on the way I had been. That was enjoyable for them. It was where they wanted me to be.

But that alone was never enough for them. In their eyes, my adolescent actions needed to be atoned for. Not atoned for as a process or a stage of life but as a permanent sign emblazoned on my forehead like a cattle brand. As enjoyable as wearing that Hester Prynne scarlet-letter billboard was, though, I knew in the minds of some I would never fully move past my youthful mistakes.

I don't bring this up to chastise any of them for a lack of forgiveness. Those who live in bitterness exist on their own special little island of darkness. It's not my issue. Instead, I want to free up others from being owned outright by the practitioners of this destiny-squelching dark art.

Oh, you know personally of what I speak?

But You Don't Understand, Ron

Yes, I do. I know what you're holding on to. I lived there for ages. You cling to the hope that if you show them you've changed, these friends and family members will eventually embrace you.

people relate to who we were then

Sorry to be Mr. Bubble Popper, but for some of them, it might never happen.

For the terminally bitter individual, you, my friend, will have transitioned in their mind from the deplorable dirt bag of the realm to the quintessential poster child for cosmic injustice. You were not supposed to do well in life, and they won't stand for it!

The more God's work is manifested in your life, the more intensely they need you to bend to the glorious groveling plan they have for your life. For the endlessly miserable ones, your blessing and growth will harden their disdain for your redeemed life.

I've had to cast off those personal anchors on a few occasions. I don't enjoy the process or seek the opportunity. It hurts my soul. But there came a time when it was the only way not to live in their world and allow it to indefinitely sabotage mine.

Dave and the Big Guy

I want to look at a specific event in the life of David and see if you and I can get a little more clarity on how we can move beyond our past and the people that love it.

In 1 Samuel 17, David told the king of the Israelites, Saul, that he'd fight the Philistine Goliath on behalf of Israel and God. The other Israelites might have been relieved, but inside they had to be thinking Dave wouldn't even make a Cheerio-sized hamburger patty in the Goliath grinder. He had no shot. Goliath was a trained warrior, victor in countless battles. Gigantic and ferocious. So much so that, to this day, his name is synonymous with imposing, overwhelming strength.

Still, Saul said to David, "Go, and the LORD be with you." Saul also had to be thinking, "I'm really going to miss that young man. I put dibs on his lyre!"

Saul wanted to dress David for the upcoming battle in the attire Saul thought would provide David the most protection, including armor and a helmet. If David were to have any chance, it made perfect sense. History had repeatedly confirmed this truth. So David put on Saul's fighting armor. But he quickly realized it felt as natural as sandals on a trout.

So he took the armor off.

To win, David needed to wear his own clothes, and he knew it. The comfortable ones. The ones that fit. Not the ones Saul wanted him to wear.

Attire dictated by others, no matter how seemingly logical, justified, or appropriate, will always come with an agenda and, in the end, restrict your ability to warrior up for God.

Stop.

Please read that last sentence again.

Marinate for as long as you need, then continue.

Check, Please!

This reality wasn't an excuse for me to thumb my nose at the people I'd wronged. God wants me to seek forgiveness and restoration.

But I came to understand that while I'm pursuing both those goals, God isn't fond of me continuing to stroll around in the garments of perpetual penance. God's desire for me (and for you) is to remove the tunic of shame and go to battle in the comfort of my own heavenly ordained gear.

Pay the penance tab? Yes. How? Ask for forgiveness. Pray for reconciliation? Indeed. Extend an invitation to the offended where they can voice their pain? Yes, even that. But if those actions have no impact, then it is time for me to get up and leave the retribution restaurant.

And I won't even leave a tip.

Don't Get Taken Out

David won the victory for the people of Israel because he went to battle with the snazzy threads God had fashioned just for him. Common, comfortable attire.

The only thing more tragic than ignoring our spiritual call is to never walk fully in it because we allow a critical heart (or hearts) to put back on the clothes of grudging bitterness that Christ removed from us when we surrendered fully to him. There is simply too much at stake for me and you to forever feel the need to appease the seething rants of the perma-peeved.

(Hint: Be mindful that often the most unforgiving people in your life can be those closest to you.)

If I let the Sauls of this world continue to dress me, I will be compliant—forever uncomfortable and restricted, but still compliant. But if I dress in my ordained comfy-ness, I can rock the giant.

Rock the giant! Get it?

I crack myself up.

The Bible is filled with men and women who were dynamic, head-strong, timid, impulsive, hesitant, and—at times—anything but compliant. The metaphorical, circumstantial, and literal giants in the Bible were not often slain by those who shrunk back in historical shame. The giants in the Bible were vanquished by the people who were willing to trust God, even when all conventional wisdom screamed, "Wear Saul's armor!"

Punt the Penance

The freedom I experienced overseas? God showed me I needed to bring that freedom back with me and walk without the restraints of historical missteps. I was not built to live in a world of endless regret or shame, no matter who wants me to. I shouldn't need to remove myself from the memory of my previous life to live in the freedom of the new.

And who's the new me? I am a man of honor. I am a loving and faithful spouse to one woman. I am a pastor, protector, and provider to my family. I am a child of the one true God.

new identity

My past is my past, and I won't run from it. I will not cover my tracks. But neither will my past define me. It's the old me. My previous life. If I'm still drawing breath, everything that happened before this very second *is* my previous life.

I once saw a meme with Johnny Depp wearing his Jack Sparrow garb. The caption read, "I don't know how to act my age. I've never been this old before."

I think that's how we should live our lives in Jesus. If we've sincerely repented, sought the appropriate forgiveness, and turned from the old us, we need to punt the penance. And if necessary, the people who forever demand it from us. I know, it hurts my foot just to think about it. But it might be what Jesus is leading us into. I can still pray for them and love them, but I needed to stop allowing them unrestricted access to my heart and hurt.

You and I can be the Christians we were meant to be. The ones we've dreamed of being. And we can do it from our couch, back yard, neighborhood, family cabin, grocery store, or workplace.

The freedom of being in another country, of being an unknown quantity to those around me, was important for me. I felt something I didn't know I could. It gave me a taste of what God has said I can live in at all times.

Freedom.

That was the real souvenir I was to bring home and display.

You and I don't need to go to a country where no one knows us for us to walk comfortably in our own salvation skin. We don't need to seek a new group of friends to experience a clean slate. The slate is already clean enough to eat off of. White as snow, right? If we want people to know that our redeemer lives, we don't have to do anything more than live our lives as though we are redeemed.

The wisest and safest place I can be is in the garments God himself created for me. We all need to set the audacious warrior inside of us free. Shake off the hand-me-down tunics of your past. They will never offer a range of motion that allows any of us who call Jesus Lord the freedom to be victorious.

Live in freedom. It's okay. We were meant to.

Put that in your hot-dog bun and relish it.

Don't be compliant. Rock the giant.

.... Shun Common ....

Chapter: The Savior in Stereo
Location: Over the Atlantic Ocean Again
Purpose: Varied

I was flying over the Atlantic Ocean to Europe. It was a multi-destination trip so I wouldn't be in any one place long. Introductory meetings always make me feel like I'm pitching Amway. Same script, same endgame, only the faces change. I want them to want my concept and products. Such a silly, desperate life I've carved out for myself. But hey . . . it's a living!

Maybe I should feel a kinship with Europe since my ancestry originates there, but I don't. To me, Europe always seemed like a rich, pompous, and humorless uncle. It's fun to see all the old stuff in his house but I wouldn't want to live there or visit very often.

My dislike—um, ambivalence (I like that better) toward Europe is in part based on my personal opposition to the idea of monarchy, royal families, and noble bloodlines. Not all Europe subscribes to these ideals but a handful of countries still cling to them.

It's an effective form of government but with it comes the belief that some people are inherently superior to others. I find that entertaining. After a lifetime of watching the European royalty on the national news, I'm pretty sure a solid case could be made against the idea of superiority.

Nevertheless, Jesus pines for their company and that should be enough for me.

Should be.

Baby steps, Ron.

And Then There Is Peter

Peter, on the other hand, seems like the polar opposite of the fictional Uncle Europe I described. From what I can see in the Bible, Peter wasn't a big fan of diplomacy or passivism. He was a no-nonsense kind of guy. Peter always comes across as a strapping, bison-like, straight-up, man-gland of a fellow. All bull, no bull, noble.

ugh

(See what I did there?) ✓

Although I'm not a rough-and-tumble fisherman like he was, I look forward to meeting him one of these days. I'm sure I'll like him a whole lot.

I enjoy that God allows Scripture to be incredibly general in some areas so I can imagine the dynamics of a story and let it soak into my spirit in a way that would be most impactful to me personally. I so love Peter's response to Jesus when they first meet in Luke 5 because I can just hear how they've been crammed with salty intensity and then triple soaked in a brash-brine. With Peter especially, reading between the lines of dialogue is thoroughly enjoyable for me.

I'm as certain as I can be that, without knowing him, Peter was not a big fan of titles or honorifics either. I agree with Peter. To me, titles always seem archaic and backward.

Some countries still have scads of them, though. I'll pick on the United Kingdom since they're on my itinerary; they speak English and the actual titles will make more sense. But they're certainly not alone when it comes to this type of vernacular. In no particular order, king, queen, duke, duchess, baron, baroness, Bert, prince, princess, lord, lady, Ernie, sir. Those are just a handful of the titles still used in UK parlance.

As I said, I'm as certain as I can be that the idea of lofty titles stuck in Peter's craw . . . except in Luke 5. Even though Peter and I are usually on the same page, on this one the story exposed a title-wave of an attitude in me that was not at all productive. In fact, it exposed more than my unfortunate 'tude. It exposed the danger and possible sin in my stance on titles.

I saw an area of my heart that I had resisted relinquishing to Christ. God doesn't change, but unfortunately I needed to in order to be more like him.

It's complicated.

As You Wish . . .

Here are the high points of the exchange between Peter and Jesus in Luke 5.

Jesus is preaching to a crowd of people when he suddenly decides to go stand in Peter's boat. Interesting. He asks Peter, who at the time was washing his nets, to push out a little from shore so he can preach from the water. Inconvenient.

There's no indication Peter said anything while he did what Jesus asked. Knowing what we know of Peter, don't you think that he had to be eyeballing Jesus a little? I do. Peter knew Jesus was a Jew and a teacher of some acclaim but he probably didn't know a lot more at that point. Based on his social status alone, Peter most likely just bit his lip. Inside, however, he had to be a tad bent about Jesus's request. Who could blame him? He was done fishing for the day. He had to be exhausted. And now this guy!

Ah, Peter . . . I feel your pain, buddy. He commandeers my life-boat all the time.

Once Jesus was done preaching, he instructed Peter to push out into deeper waters and let out his nets. Intrusive. Here is where I can feel Peter pushing back a little. Inside his rather ample belly (yeah, I'm guessing, but go with me on this) he had to be losing his patience with this Jesus guy.

To boldly put words in Peter's mouth, or head, I think he wanted to say, "Oh, okay, big-time *carpenter* guy, please school me on how to do my lifelong vocation and, while you're at it, make me look like a dirt-eating dolt in front of my peers. I'm tired and irritable, and my knuckles need to find a worthy chin."

To his credit, what Peter said is, "Master, we've worked hard all night and haven't caught anything. But because you say so, I will let down the nets." Peter didn't even point out that the nets were freshly washed and this would require them to be washed all over again. I might have.

When he let down his nets, they became so full of fish that they tore. This was not just a really big bunch of fish in his nets; this was a humongous haul of fish, enough so that Peter immediately recognized the catch as a miracle from God. Peter fell at Jesus's feet and said, "Go away from me, Lord; I am a sinful man!"

Did you catch it? Did you notice Peter's heart transformation? It's there.

When Jesus first instructed Peter to push out into deeper water and let down his nets, Peter did so and called Jesus "master." But after Jesus met Peter in his own world with a clear miracle, Peter called him "Lord." There was something more than a little fishy going on here.

I kept reading this exchange between Jesus and Peter over and over again. I knew I was missing something in this story that had my name on it. When it finally hit me, I could feel it churning in my gut. If I had drunk a glass of milk at that moment, it would have quickly turned into butter.

In Peter's initial response to Jesus, he called him master. After Jesus had met Peter in a very personal way, on his own professional turf, Peter called him Lord. That was it. I was completely comfortable calling Jesus master. I like the way it flowed and felt. But Jesus as Lord, in the truest sense of the word, was a subtle problem for me.

As usual, I was a complete mess. (Attention shoppers, I need a cleanup on aisle me.)

My Issue?

Master in the Greek used in Luke 5 is a title that means "teacher, knowledge holder." When Peter referred to Jesus as *master*, he was recognizing Jesus as a rabbi and a good moral teacher, in much the same way other religions portray him. It was a title of positional respect.

But when Peter calls Jesus *Lord*, this is the word that slaves in his day would have used to refer to their owners. In this exchange, Peter is saying, "Sir, I don't know exactly what it is about you, but you are a force to be reckoned with and obviously wield some serious supernatural mojo! I don't know who you are. I only know that I have no place in your world."

I was fine thinking of Jesus as Dr. Jesus, PhD of my heart. But coming to grips with Jesus as the one who demanded my complete and utter dependence on him was harder than I thought.

Instructor? Hey, Jesus is my friend, right? I can deal with that.

Utter dependence? There must be another way.

"Complete surrender" was for the weak. I didn't like the connotations associated with the term or the pride-swallowing resignation it required.

How rebellious am I? I'm not sure if it's measurable by existing technology.

Sir Ronald of Nothing-ham

I had allowed my opposition to royalty and their lofty titles to seep into my relationship with Jesus. Or maybe it was always there and this was Jesus performing a cr-appendectomy on my innards. Either way, it was toxic and I needed it removed.

How many Lord miracles and God moments have I missed out on because of my unwillingness to relinquish all that I am? I honor him as rabbi and teacher but spit the bit when it comes to him being my absolute everything. I needed a Peter-like transformation.

Hopefully, without the fish.

Crank It Up

So, let's discuss car stereo systems. I want to talk about them to make my secondary point. I'm also shooting for a seemingly illogical and clunky transition. It's a present for you. Don't mention it.

While driving the other day, I heard a commercial for a car stereo retailer. They asked, "Does your car stereo sound like this [basic rock music plays], or does it sound like this [louder, fuller rock music plays]?"

Huh? How pointless is that? They want me to judge their car stereo system based on hearing an example of it on my car stereo! If it sounded bad on my stereo, why would I want their stereo system? If it sounded fantastic on my stereo system, why would I need their stereo system? There is no way for me to compare what I have with what they are offering without hearing it firsthand.

The same thing holds true for me as a Christian.

The lordship of Jesus Christ can only be fully experienced in person, through the crystal clear, righteous tunes of my own acknowledging surrender. His lordship over me cannot be experienced vicariously, by default, or through the distortion of an alternative spiritual sound system. Nobody else can describe what it feels like for me to meet Jesus as Lord. Nobody else's sound system will do it justice.

It was so simple but so tough to get a bead on this truth. I connected the faint dots of my sneaky sin and repented. His sufficiency is all I count as genuine gain now. I like it there. I should have no place in his world and yet somehow I do.

Regardless of my dislike for man-made, European titles, Jesus is the only one worthy of the titles *master* and *Lord*, and my unqualified acknowledgment of both.

Ask Peter. He caught it.

·············· Shun Common ···

Chapter: Sowing Machines

Location: It's a Secret

Purpose: Annual Budget Talks

This story is a harsh one.

Thought you might appreciate the warning. But I can't forget its impact on me, so I'm going to tell it to you. And I'm going to make a friend of mine seem a little creepy. So I'm not going to use his name. (Makes me feel so good to go skipping down the honorable cobblestones.)

I feel strongly enough about protecting this individual that I'm not even going to tell you the name of the country this experience took place in. (*Cough*—chopsticks—*cough*.) I don't think the story loses its relevance if you, the reader, don't know the exact area of the world where this event took place. (Godzilla. *Ahem*.) I hope you can respect my decision not to be too specific. Sushi—er, sorry.

On this particular business trip, his wife was close to full term with their second child. A girl.

You'd never know it based on our schedule.

At noon, he received notification that his wife was in labor and at the hospital. The interest needle on this guy didn't budge. At five thirty, he was told that the child had been born. Ambivalence oozed from his eyes. At seven, he was informed that the child was ill and there was concern about her survival. Still no emotional pulse. It wasn't the fact that he continued to casually discuss business that I found so unsettling. It was that any other topic seemed to irritate him. Like it got in the way. Hello? Anyone answering the "do something" bell?

There were six of us at that conference table that evening, but I couldn't tell you how a single one of them reacted to the reports we were getting. I couldn't take my eyes off this man. I desperately wanted to see

113

the concern of a father on his face. A crack in the stoic armor. Shoulders slumped. A deep sigh. Anything!

Finally, at eight thirty, we loaded into a car and headed for the hospital. When we arrived, we piled out and my friend led us to the entrance. I said I'd wait outside but was told I should come with them. A hospital attendant led us to a stark, abrasively lit room with a stainless steel table in the center of it.

The room was as inviting as a crypt.

We waited in uncomfortable, sterile silence. Had the baby died? Why was I there? Was this the place they brought people to tell them the news this atmosphere of antiseptic death had already emotionally prepped them for?

Then the door on the other side of the room opened and a nurse came in holding a tiny, pink-blanketed bundle. She was alive. I jumped up and down a little bit, inside. My friend didn't flinch. The nurse laid the bundle on the cold metal table. As we watched, the nurse undid the blanket until the little girl lay naked. So sick she couldn't even muster a cry. The nurse took one step back and my friend took one step forward. He stared at this tiny little girl for a few seconds, nodded stoically, then turned and left. Dumbfounded, I followed.

It felt like he had just nodded his approval to a pork chop in a deli case.

Now all of us carried a look of concerned compassion—except my friend. He wanted to go get something to eat.

Really? How could anyone think about food at a time like this? Did he think this persona made him look strong or macho? The whole experience left me cold and kind of hacked off.

After a quick meal, we drove back to the office to wind up our business discussions. Still shocked, I contributed very little to the conversation. Near the end of our meeting, quite suddenly, my friend stood up, leaned over the conference table, and—with the delicate, tender hands of a neurosurgeon—carefully picked up a gnat that had landed on the table. Cradling the gnat, he slowly walked to the window, opened it, and gently released the insect into the cool night air. I kid you not.

Um . . . huh?

What the diaper bag was that! I thought, *You looked at your own flesh and blood, your newborn daughter, your gravely ill baby girl, like she just stole your car. But a gnat, a cruddy little gnat with a gazillion nasty bacteria swimming on it and a phonetically dumb name—you lavish it with a level of concern and attention that would shame a diamond cutter.*

I didn't speak up. I stayed silent. To my shame. The entire event still bothers me.

Where am I going with this? Stay with me. We're getting there. But we're going to digress for a moment. It'll be worth it, I promise. (Please, Lord, let it be worth it.)

Sow What?

"They're gonna reap what they sow."

Most of the time when I hear that phrase uttered, people mean bad things are certain to sucker punch bad people. They use the phrase as if it's a magical spiritual truth that, when spoken, somehow transforms the dove of the Holy Spirit into a flock of pigeons circling endlessly above the offender's freshly washed carnal car.

I confess, I often want this to be true. I wanted it to be true for my friend. I want cruel people to feel the swift return of the bad-choice boomerang as I stroll around my own private amusement park of misguided satisfaction. I watch with sordid pleasure as the stalks of skunk cabbage break the swampy soil of those who have sown poorly in their lives.

Oh, you've done the same thing? Thank you. Whew! I'm not alone.

But let me ask you, why are we so consumed with watching (and secretly hoping for) the negative consequences of people planting the wrong kind of seed? Our lives, our spirits, aren't enriched by this observation, are they?

The Reason We Stare

Often we use the sowing-and-reaping binoculars on others so we don't have to witness the consequences of what we're tossing into the fertile ground of our lives.

Pretty handy self-distraction tool, don't you think?

I think Christians can be described as bread-and-wine-powered sowing machines that are always running—whether we're sowing good seed or bad.

It's pretty obvious what good seed looks like. Grace. Encouragement. Love. Seeds sown in a staccato cadence of grace, encouragement, and love should be the norm. We should be sowing seeds that empower believers and nonbelievers to flourish in their unique abilities and calling.

I like being esteemed more than esteeming others. I like talking much more than listening. I want to be noticed, praised, thought well of, adored. (Can anyone say "self-absorbed"? Yes, thank you, sir, I see that hand way in the back.)

I have glanced at the two bags of seed on my hip and too often chosen the one that has a rich variety of poison ivy and noxious weeds. And I've spread them on not only my land but also the land of others, because the land is all connected.

The consequences of the seeds we toss, good or bad, are never solitary. They do what plants do: they spread.

Here's Johnny!

Remember Johnny Appleseed? That guy was incredible! He introduced the apple tree to five states. How? By never staying in one spot too long. If he'd remained in one of those five states long enough to see the trees sprout and grow to beautiful maturity, he would have never made the impact he did on a much larger region.

If we're sowing seeds in the lives of family or close friends, we should nurture those seeds and tend them as a farmer would. But if our seeds go out to the world at large, we should scatter them and trust God with their growth and care. Wanting to always see the results of our seed sowing will seriously restrict the territory we bring life to. Seeing the fruit grow to maturity should be considered a rare blessing from God and not a right of ownership.

I realize that giving away possessions and sowing encouragement and life to get richer makes as much sense as engaging in a Pizza Rolls and

Twinkie diet to fit into your high school jeans. Sometimes I wish I were not emotionally hamstrung by any of this pesky, faith-based, counter-intuitive smarm. But my spirit tells me that abundant life can be found in this stuff.

I Missed My Opportunity with My Not-So-Mysterious Friend

I want you to understand where I blew it badly with my Japanese friend. I sowed anger and disdain for him. I wanted to see his train wreck. And I'm sure by the end of the evening he knew that with certainty.

At times like that, I love the Ten Commandments and the Law. Big fan.

The Beatitudes? Not so much.

I had an opportunity to speak life to him and I failed. Miserably. I thought I was exhibiting a righteous, holy anger. Not the case. I was too busy being the judge and jury. I was okay leaving the actual execution to God, but I really wanted to observe it.

As I said, big fan.

I missed my chance to tell my friend what a stunningly beautiful daughter he has. How strong she was. How she would bring honor to him. I should have told him how his actions toward the gnat spoke of his concern for life and that I admired that about him. I should have told him something. Anything.

I just realized that I've left you hanging without a crucial bit of information! Sorry about that. His daughter survived her illness and, I understand from others, grew to be a young woman who embodies the attributes of which I just spoke. Rest easy.

My Life Ledger

I don't always need to connect the dots for people. That's God's job. I don't need to bludgeon people with truth.

Truth, spoken in love, sets people free.

Truth, spoken with malice, can divide and maim people.

I chose to silently seethe and hope for bad things in my friend's life.

I was so consumed with my own sense of gnat-smashing injustice that I wasted an opportunity to interject Jesus. The horrific duplicity of his actions was teed up perfectly for me to gently highlight with words of grace. Me? I angrily shanked it into the woods.

The chance to talk to this man about his daughter never presented itself again. Like it or not, it's now part of my story and I can't shake it. I'm no longer angry about his actions, just repentant about mine.

Sowing the seeds of grace, life, and mercy is a daily commitment to hope and redemption. Gleefully or angrily monitoring the results of other people's transgressions is a daily surrender to despair and loathing. I don't want to squander those life-changing moments any longer.

So I lost my injustice ledger, loosened my grip, and started slinging seeds! Good ones.

You in?

Shun Common

Chapter: The Monologue of Discourse

Location: Istanbul, Turkey

Purpose: Licensing Agreement

I'm 99.8 percent certain (at least in that neighborhood) of the deity of Jesus Christ and that the Bible is the inerrant Word of God. Shocked? Too bad.

Yes, I would like to be one-hundred-percent certain—but I'm not.

I know this kind of confession makes some people spew beverages from their noses. But if I were one-hundred-percent certain of every single facet of my faith, it wouldn't be called faith. Consider the following as you pray for my soul.

faith

The Pendulum Principle

All of us know that unless a swinging pendulum is artificially propelled it will systematically lose velocity. With every downward and then upward arc of the pendulum, gravity will pull it in a lower and lower arc until it extends straight down and is without movement.

Now imagine you're lying face down on a scaffolding twenty feet off the ground. Only your face extends over the edge of the plank. Just barely touching your nose is a two-hundred-pound weight. That weight is attached to a cable and the cable is attached to a fulcrum somewhere above you. As you lay there motionless, feeling the cold metal of the weight against your nose, you hear a lever release and watch as the weight falls away from you to begin its path down and then up the other side.

Your eyes widen as the weight begins its return arc toward you.

As it approaches your face, do you flinch? Do you shut your eyes? Do you pull your head up? Does your heart race? Is there a very real moment of anxiety?

You would do some, maybe all, of those things? What? I don't understand. I thought you understood the principle of a pendulum. Why all
the flinching and anxiety? (I'd, of course, be right there with you!)

Anyone faced with this situation would recoil from the weight. It's
easy to know and trust a principle like that of the pendulum when I have
nothing to risk. Trust in the principle vanishes, though, when it's my
nose on the line. When I am faced with a compelling force, much of what
I think I know is not as certain as I'd like people to believe.

Flinching Among Friends

Allow me to tell you about a time I danced the tightrope of uncertainty.

It happened during a conversation in Istanbul, Turkey. The man I was
talking with was learned and articulate about Islam, a faith he believed
in as much as I believed in my Christianity. We had covered our business
topics in short order and felt comfortable enough to dive into other sub-
jects. The conversation was animated and enjoyable. I liked this guy a
lot. We compared points of agreement about the creation, the prophets,
and the significant events of the Old Testament. With very few excep-
tions, we found common ground in our understanding and beliefs.

But before we got to the New Testament and the subject of Jesus, he
stopped and pointed a finger at me. "Islam, unlike Christianity, is based
on fact, not debatable events or superstition," he said.

Okay. That was random. The directness of it took me off guard.

I don't like presuppositions like that. They choke off genuine communication. But hey, I'm not going anywhere, so let's do this. Gauntlet
thrown. Minor flinch? You bet.

You with me on this one?

Inside I bristled (just a hair). On the outside I smiled and nodded
my interest in continuing the conversation. And we did—till we hit the
crucifixion.

No surprise there. The cross never ceases to put a significant wrinkle
in any conversation.

The man smoothly and confidently said: "But Isa [Jesus Christ] did

not die on the cross. God replaced him with an identical-looking man
who died in his place. God took Jesus up to himself that day."

As he started in on his next thought, I raised my hand in polite protest. "Excuse me," I said, "I thought Islam was based on fact?"

He looked at me like I had just asked whether or not he had webbed
feet and gills.

Before he could get to full steam again, I continued. "Muhammad
made that proclamation about Jesus not actually dying on the cross
over six hundred years after the crucifixion. Coming up with a story that
contradicts all historical reports to the contrary over the previous six
hundred years is not a fact."

I could sense him recoiling. Boom! Now who's flinching? That was a
fun moment. (As I told you before, I recall my conversational victories
more clearly than my defeats.)

He sat back and forced his own uneasy smile. The point had been
made and we both knew it.

Had we not been friends, I don't think the rest of the conversation
would have been quite so pleasant. In the end, though, the respect
between us grew and we deepened our genuine appreciation for the mind
and convictions of the other. That respect for one another has endured.

Not all conversations go this way. Other worldviews have their own
set of verbally defensible doctrines, complete with recorded miracles
and anecdotal assurances. If you're not ready for the tussle, you can get
your hind end handed to you. It's happened to me on more than one
occasion.

Shhhh. Don't tell anyone.

Lose the 'Tude

If I were one-hundred-percent confident my beliefs were unequivo-
cally true, any open exchange of ideas would never unnerve or bother
me. But I have been unnerved and bothered at times. You too? I've been
presented with highly defensible worldviews that differ greatly from my
own. When the pendulum of a seemingly well-reasoned, contrary faith
has approached my nose, I have at times flinched.

I don't perceive this as a weakness. I view it as one of my greatest assets.

Am I saying what I hold as truth can be swayed by every convincing wind of doctrine or nose-crunching logic?

Um, no! Remember, 99.8 percent!

But isn't embracing this tiny doubt the only honest way to engage people with whom I disagree but wish to call brothers and sisters in Christ?

You might get the impression I see my faith as a relationally dominated wind sprint that is always on the edge of plunging off the cliff. Not the case. Even though I believe no mutual quest for truth can take place without a willingness to exchange and consider, I also believe any thorough examination of truth will confirm Jesus as the risen Lord and Savior.

The bottom line? I refuse to engage in a window-dressing debate with an unreachable attitude and arrogance that lurks just below the surface.

I was made in God's image. I was not asked to make God into the image of my knowledge, politics, heritage, friends, or cultural familiarity.

Not So Different

Over the years, I've become friends with many amazing people. Among the many was a Muslim man of North African heritage. Near the end of one of my trips to see him, he and I talked alone.

I mean really talked.

I think my understanding of the Old Testament surprised him, and we both realized that the other's faith, although different, was not as violent or haphazard as we might have previously thought.

As we talked, he grew serious and I sensed he wanted to pose a difficult question. Head down, he quietly said, "Sometimes I am not so sure. Sometimes I have doubts about my faith. Do you ever feel this way?"

Without hesitating, I said, "Of course I do. He's a gigantic God."

And by gigantic I mean he-spoke-the-galaxies-into-being-and-his-ways-are-so-very-clearly-not-mine kind of *huge*. For example, I can't wrap my mind around the flood. Drowning is incredibly high on the list of most people's greatest fear. Why was it necessary for everyone to die in such a terrifying way? Couldn't God have just stopped everyone's heart at the same time, then flooded the earth so all the metaphors of cleansing and baptism were still intact? I can't square the event with my perception of God.

Or why the drawn-out, horrific nature of the crucifixion? The death, burial, and resurrection were the only aspects required to redeem a lost world. I understand the fulfillment of the prophesies, but those also could have been different to reflect a simplified event and still accomplish his will. For me, the massive injustice of God dying at the hands of those he came to save is not strengthened by the long and terrible process of it. Just the fact that he died for me is enough.

On these issues and others, I have come to the conclusion that God was, and is, working out his love for a lost world in the most perfect way possible. I just can't grasp it.

Oswald Chambers once said, "Faith is deliberate confidence in the character of God whose ways you may not understand at the time." That was it. That thought was enough for me to bridge the gap. Besides, I have enough problems living out the portions of Scripture that I think I understand completely.

With my admission of uncertainty, all the walls fell between me and my North African friend. After that, we spoke of the deepest things two people can discuss. We discussed the Trinity and other theological differences between our faiths. His sincerity and lively mind still warm my heart when I think back on our time together. His reasoning was flinchworthy. We both flinched. We both laughed, scoffed, playfully chided, agreed, and disagreed.

It was so good and spiritually edifying for me. Regardless of any niggling disconnects in my finite mind, my Jesus could hold his own, even with me as his mouthpiece. That time was a rare treasure for me and, for his sake, I will take some of what we discussed to my grave.

If you struggle from time to time, it's okay to admit it. Really. It's okay to question. It's okay to wake up in the middle of the night when the only sound you hear is your heart pounding as you wonder if any of this faith business is true.

Jesus is not offended. If you seek him, you will find him—even in the heart of Istanbul. A stunningly beautiful city, by the way. Who knew Jesus hung out there?

Do You Want Others to Hear You?

The only thing that can be clearly heard over the din of dogma is an open and honest spirit diligently thirsting for truth.

This has to be about truth. It can never be about arrogance. Truth-seeking and arrogance are not good roommates. Our pride doesn't attest to our actual level of understanding. We need to decide why we are in the debate. Seriously. Do we want to see people introduced to the real Jesus Christ, or do we just want to sound intelligent and look confident?

I believe that my willingness to engage anyone with an open spirit is how my Savior will ultimately reveal himself to those I want to meet Jesus and call friends in Christ. None of us has all the answers, and acting like we do shrinks God down to the size of our embarrassing arrogance.

For me, it's not really an issue of certainty; it's more an issue of clarity. All things considered, I'm pretty happy with 99.8 percent.

In fact, I like my odds a whole lot.

············· Shun Common ···

For some, this chapter will likely skewer a sacred cow. Maybe more. Admittedly, that's fun for me, but I like you, so I figured I should give at least a casual warning in case you're not quite as contrarian as I am.

What I Like

I love the unique way Germans use their language. The Germans will create a single word to convey a complex or specific emotion. My favorite new words are *zeitgeist* (it means "the defining spirit or mood of a particular period of history as shown by the ideas and beliefs of the time"— love that) and *schadenfreude* ("pleasure derived by someone from another person's misfortune"; I confess, when it comes to politicians, I'm so very, very guilty of schadenfreude).

Frankfurt, Germany, of any place I've ever been, might be the best example of modern industrial design. The airport is clean and impressive and has all the warmth and charm of Superman's Fortress of Solitude. I've never seen so much concrete, glass, stainless steel, and cable in one structure.

Some people love it. It's just not my style. It's no surprise, really. It's kind of what I expected. The German people in urban areas are known to be precise, measured, and somewhat stoic. They are tremendous engineers but, as a collective, not the bubbliest herd on the planet.

The architecture fits the people. It reflects the cumulative population of Frankfurt. Even the prewar buildings here appear more imposing and impressive than they do majestic and inspiring.

Nobody would say that the people of Frankfurt adopted specific personality traits to reflect the buildings they constructed. That wouldn't make sense. The people of Frankfurt built the structures according to their collective taste and temperament. The buildings reflect the people that created them, not the other way around.

In America we're a melting pot so our architecture is more diversified. Mutt huts. Influences from many countries can be recognized in our structures. We tend to make our personal dwellings the place we focus on to represent our taste and style. My wife and I love a Pacific Northwest Craftsman style. Friends of ours love a farmhouse feel to their home. Others tend toward more modern expressions. Victorian- and Tudor-style homes are still popular in the Seattle area.

Very few people buy or build a style of home they don't genuinely dig. Like the German people, we create atmospheres that fall in line with our own unique tastes. It's a uniquely human quality.

We all good with these assumptions?

What Makes Us Tick, Talk

I recently took a personality and strengths test. I'm not sure if I learned much new stuff about myself or even wanted to. I took it mostly to appease a pastor friend of mine, knowing full well my results might confuse him more than give him insight into my psyche.

Ah, the things I do for entertainment!

Fitting into a standard temperament evaluation has not been a particularly clean process for me. The way I talk reflects my personality as much as it does my heart. My personality is an unusual hybrid of both Lassie and Cujo. I crave relationship and community but routinely seek to lone-wolf it when it comes to business and challenges. I can be engaging and playful at times and quiet and reserved at others. I routinely and willingly place myself in the life-of-the-party role but I'm terrified of speaking in front of crowds.

Surprised? I knew you wouldn't be. God didn't break the mold after making me. I'm pretty sure the mold was broken beforehand.

I took a much simpler personality test many years ago that was based on bodily fluids, mostly bile—no, I'm not kidding. Not the most flattering barometer. There were only four primary personality categories. It seemed pretty limited and, to be truthful, a little disgusting. (Bile is a corrosive acid, yes? I sure hope bile is not the means God uses to sort us out.)

Given that an infinitely creative God fashioned all of us, I tend to believe that individuals are infinitely unique as well. As it is with cities, so it is with people. All created things are in some part a reflection of the one that created them.

What's the Point?

I think the purpose of all such tests is to identify what stirs our individual cocoa and why. If we can recognize and operate in our God-given strengths, we should be more effective in life, relationships, and ministry.

Simple enough, I guess. But it's hard to take such a test and come away with the understanding that God obviously put some thought into us. We're not zombies or honeybee drones. To be honest, I need that truth. Without it, I'm not sure there would be enough godly gravy in the ladle to make my personality potato palatable, or so I've heard. My wife and kids like me, though! And you're still reading this hot mess—so, there's that.

Everyone I know who's recently taken the Myers-Briggs test seems genuinely excited about the self-discovery. With the knowledge it provides, they can fine-tune their service to others based on how they were emotionally designed. When we understand the reason we do what we do and think the way we think, it can be a game changer.

Snow Globes

I don't like to rain on my own pathology parade, but why do I think my God-breathed inclinations end at spiritual gifting or my taste in architecture and trappings?

If I'm honest, every church I've felt truly committed to falls in line with what I find comfortable. Most of us wind up at the type of church that clicks with us internally. We find churches that are in line with our unique personalities. I also quite naturally gravitate toward churches that engage in a style of worship that's consistent with how God made me. Like the architecture, it seems logical and obvious, doesn't it?

So why am I convinced those who don't share my style of praise and worship are somehow off base, not as enlightened, or missing out? I strut around inside my snow globe of superiority, totally oblivious to the tiny, God-suffocating world I call home. It's a big world and a big church, people.

We need to break the glass and choose people over preference.

If another person is not drawn deeper into worship by raising their hands, does that mean that God created them less able to touch his heart? If a follower of Jesus likes to dance and wave flags, does that mean they can't experience the Father in a deep and intimate way? Why do we—why do I—believe these things?

I think we all need to order up a double tall get-over-ourselves mocha.

Slow the Madness

Transparency moment: churches that sing three hymns at preordained points in the service are almost painful for me to sit through. You might as well hook up a Shop-Vac to my innermost being and suck my soul out.

Conversely, worship services that resemble a ticker-tape parade bewilder me. I want to sneak out and pump a sedative gas through the ventilation system to calm them down.

Truth is, that's not my style and that's just fine.

There are people, devout followers of Christ, in those congregations who are totally engaged by those forms of praise and worship. It's how they glorify God. (Within reason, of course. Snake handlers, I'm eyeballin' you here.) Just because those styles of worship don't simmer my gumbo doesn't automatically mean those worshippers are missing out or are somehow unhinged.

Because we're all unique in how God crafted us, we will always have inclinations toward specific forms of dwellings, services, social interactions, and, yes, even worship. Try as we might, we cannot see our worship without viewing it through the lens of our own individual temperament and preferences.

Here's the rub. To assume that your personal preferences, when it comes to praise and worship, are exclusively representative of the heart of God is, in my opinion, absurdly arrogant.

We're all not that hip and a bag of chips.

To fully enter into the Holy of Holies and kneel at the feet of the Almighty is a process of obedience, acknowledgment, and surrender. No amount of solemn piety will determine the sincerity or depth of my worship, and no degree of physical manifestations will authenticate my praise.

Clone Wars

I introduced the bile example and feel compelled to end with it. Bile is an acid. It's a corrosive fluid that eats away at most organic material.

If I hold my specific style of worship as the primary model by which God is glorified, my heart of worship is self-serving and, quite possibly, highly corrosive to the body of Christ. I will never be the end-all of praise. I'm not the standard by which true worship is judged.

I need to do what resonates with me but also allow others the latitude to respond as God made them.

Yes, I should be open to more and deeper expressions of praise and worship. But that's God's responsibility to nurture and impart into me and others, not mine. For the sake of people, God's people, I need to let them be the unique creatures they were created to be. I need to trust God with the hearts and hands of those who diligently seek him.

Worship edifies the people but doesn't create the structure itself. His people create the atmosphere and structure of worship.

Live in the zeitgeist of worship, not the schadenfreude of faith. Sing and praise in spirit and truth.

Friend or Foe

As followers of Jesus, styles of worship are not the galleons that we should be squandering our cannonballs on. That only sinks vessels and maims people. The sole purpose of that type of conflict is to glorify one-self and those of like mind while undermining that which is different.

What a waste.

God is more than capable of moving in the hearts of *all* his people. If he needs our assistance, I'm sure he'll let us know.

Stow the cannons while you're in the harbor of harbors. Remember, it's called "worship," not "warship."

············   *Shun Common*   ···

Chapter: Butterfingers or Milky Way
Location: Cairo, Egypt
Purpose: Sourcing Supply Channels

My wife and I were in Cairo, Egypt, testing and approving products to be used in the coffee shops we were preparing to open there. Yes, they drink coffee in Egypt, the land of pyramids and grave robbers, and I dig that. (That was an archaeological quip.)

The company I was dealing with specialized in sourcing products and systems for foreign companies expanding into the Egyptian market. We were presented with numerous paper cups and other consumables to consider. The conversation was enjoyable and progress was being made. These were Coptic Christians and their spiritual beliefs were much closer to my own than the average Egyptian.

A few days later, our host suddenly perked up and asked us if we wanted to meet someone special. "Sure!" we said. We were escorted through a labyrinth of hallways until we reached a nondescript beige door.

I don't recall what I expected to see on the other side of the door, but it wasn't an unassuming twentysomething woman. She looked pleasant and smiled warmly enough so I ruled out the possibility of scarabs pouring out of her eyes and mouth. (Me thinketh I watch too many movies.) She turned in her chair and rose to greet us. I don't recall her name; I only recall wondering what all the fuss was about.

It was explained to us that this young woman was of one-hundred-percent pure Egyptian blood. Being your average, run-of-the-mill American mongrel, I was less than impressed by her initial zygote status.

This wasn't a tuba-playing narwhal or a hobbit giving pedicures. It was a young lady at a computer. The phrase "big stinking deal" was close to rolling off my ill-advised tongue. The reason I plugged up my piehole was because, to them, it was clear I should be feeling at least a modicum of awe.

As I came to understand, this young woman represented a completely undiluted lineage of Egyptian ancestry. The legacy it represented was revered by them. Honored. Obviously, a pure bloodline in Egypt was more important than it was in Seattle. I didn't get it but shared their celebration of this young woman as much as my understanding allowed.

It made me wonder why their ancestry, their legacy, was so important to them (and to many other cultures around the world) but all but absent from my emotional lexicon.

Does a Goldfish Have a Pelvis?

I was forced to concede that I seldom think about my legacy, or my heritage for that matter.

Do you think about yours? If you do, you're in a decided minority. Not many of us do these days. I tend to be much more fixated on the now, on living in the moment, and any serious consideration of what I pass on after my death has never taken up much of my brain space. Previous generations did. Me? I think about my extended legacy as often as a goldfish ruminates about particle accelerators.

Mind you, I'm not talking about financial inheritance or the elitist belief that some people are superior to others by virtue of what pelvis they were pulled from. I'm talking about the type of legacy that my children, grandchildren, and great-grandchildren could point to and cite as a source of foundational strength and encouragement.

The Old Testament places great emphasis on who begat whom and what historical influences shaped the prophets and people of that time. And the first book of the New Testament starts out with the genealogy of Jesus Christ.

I don't think I've ever started anything I wrote or said like that: "Ron, grandson of Ralph, son of Duke, husband of Tina, and father of Danielle and Riley."

Maybe I should. I'm thinking God's thinking it's important. So I'm thinking it should be important for me to think about.

So I did.

Birth Deflects

Many people today would have a greater chance of recalling their experience in the birth canal than they would of recounting the life of any ancestor more than two generations removed. Because of this, we seldom consider how the example we set in our lives will be remembered and influence those who come after us.

All this stuff was filtering through my mind from a simple meeting with a young Egyptian woman. And in the process, one word kept churning to the surface.

Legacy.

Legacy was my kale. I knew it was good for me but not exactly enjoyable.

A Secular Legacy Versus a Godly Legacy

A legacy only comes in two primary blood types: secular and godly. I needed to look at each. Both are fragile and tarnished by the same factors. But how they're achieved, and how they impact lives around me, is radically different.

A secular legacy often says the end justifies the means, that collateral damage is an acceptable by-product—and is even applauded if the level of power, wealth, and influence achieved is large enough. Sadly, I have been guilty of this. A secular legacy is impersonal and derives its value in contrast with anything around it. A secular legacy is like a spotlight used to attract attention to a store's grand opening or a Hollywood event. The light is harsh and overpowers any light near it. It repels association. It serves only one purpose—to draw attention to a single point of interest.

That stings.

A godly legacy doesn't have a spotlight focused on it. It doesn't need to announce itself. A godly legacy is like the perfect campfire. You know the ones. Large enough to provide warmth to those around it but not so large it singes your arm hair when you try to roast a marshmallow. It casts the perfect amount of light to see everyone's face but isn't so bright you can see the surrounding campsites. It's inviting and cozy but not intrusive or distracting. The glow from it is strong, warm, reassuring.

You feel safe when you sit around it. Exactly like a godly legacy should make you feel.

Obviously, I had some work to do.

Polar Opposites

President Donald Trump (It Still Sounds Weird)

Donald Trump's life has been one of economic successes and failures. His life has also been punctuated by two well-publicized divorces, manicured fame, and a headlong pursuit of personal accolades and power. I can't bring myself to make fun of his hair. Talk amongst yourselves.

I changed my mind.

Besides ushering in a comb-over apocalypse, he's named buildings, a golf course, and even a board game after whom? Correct. Himself! Much of his fame is a by-product of his wealth. That's not to say the man is not business savvy or hasn't engaged in philanthropic activities. He is and he has. It's only to say that his legacy will unavoidably, and accurately, be one of excess, self-promotion, fame, fortune, and power at all cost.

Reverend Billy Graham

A personal hero of mine, Billy Graham is a man who regularly deflected attention away from himself by pointing to his Savior. His legacy is predominantly comprised of a lifetime of service to God and others.

The husband of one wife and father of five, Graham humbly accepted the unique call of God on his life. Billy Graham preached the gospel in more than 185 countries to more than 215 million people. The list of people who sought Billy Graham's company reads like a who's who of world leaders. From him they sought prayer and perspective, not fame and fortune.

One Can Be Created, the Other Can't

You can manufacture a secular legacy. I was good at all things coffee. For years I carefully crafted how I wanted to be perceived by others in the coffee industry. I saw this same process daily on my TV screen. Some of the most intellectually and ethically vacant people were held up as people we should emulate for no other reason than that they can sing, act, make money, or play a sport better than others. The echoes from this type of legacy survive the person but seldom positively influence future generations. A secular legacy defines the individual by comparing their abilities to those that come after them.

I can't manufacture a godly legacy. It happens organically. It can't be massaged or manipulated into being. If I try, it will simply slip through my butterfingers.

My Constellations

This is the mental picture I use to keep my legacy as an ongoing thing in my daily brain. It's not a doctrinal statement. Any godly legacy is a product of longevity and consistency.

Think of it this way: if I rise in the morning and fulfill my godly purpose for that day, God places a star in my legacy sky. If I do that for a week, God forms a constellation from my obedience. In a year, he will position a cluster of stars in my legacy sky. If I do it for a lifetime, God will create my Milky Way, and its beauty will defy description.

It's mostly in my head right now, but I believe it will happen. Its beauty will be in the whole of it, but the whole of it will be made up of millions of individual points of my daily choices.

"I knew it!" you say. "I told you, he's a legalist. Works. Works. Works." Oh, hush it.

Love is a choice. I'm keenly aware that I'm saved by grace and that alone is my winning Wonka Bar. I just refuse to gleefully trample the robe of his holiness in the process of walking in that grace.

I'm resolved, at the very least, that my godly legacy will not be seen exclusively as the achievement of moi. My actions alone can never raise my legacy to the level that God can elevate it to. I do pray that the gravitational pull of my legacy draws everyone around it and holds them safely in place. If my legacy is a product of my own making, however, history will always interpret it in the harshest of light. I seriously don't want that. But if my legacy is built on daily obedience, faith, and the perfect work of Christ, it will age elegantly under a glorious patina of empowering heritage.

My ancestry may not be pristine or qualify me for worldly royalty like the young Egyptian woman my wife and I met. But as long as I have my Father's heart and his Son's blood coursing through my veins, I'm good to go.

For the remainder of my days I will choose to populate my legacy sky with the stars of daily surrender. Then I'll step aside, hush up, rest in his grace, and let the God of the galaxies make it brilliant.

·············· *Shun Common* ··

Chapter: That's a Dumb Question

Location: Kyoto, Japan

Purpose: Opening a Coffee Shop

If I realized I'd lost my wallet and figured I must have left it at the baseball game I'd been at earlier that day, I wouldn't head for a different stadium to find it. I'd head for the one I'd just been at.

And when I arrived at the stadium where I'd lost my wallet, I wouldn't ask to see the botanical classification of the outfield turf. I wouldn't try to identify the mineral composition of the infield dirt or the volume of carbonated beverages sold last year. I would merely want to find my wallet, so the only questions I'd ask are ones that would help me do so.

You'd do the same?

Good, you and I are in sync.

Border Disorder

I like minutia and intricate details. Too much. I believe they provide much more context than clarity.

Much of what I've learned, and been challenged by, about my faith has arisen from the people I've met who think differently than me, not from history. Unlike people in some countries, I'm woeful at considering my past when responding to my present situation. (I've already made this abundantly clear in a few chapters.)

Some changes are hard-fought for me. I seem to be more apt to consider future ramifications when making my decisions today. At times it's me exercising wisdom. Other times it's me being a manipulative troglodyte. A godly balance between my past and my future often eludes me. But I'm getting better at it.

I'm not trying to be critical of other cultures for their reverence of history. It's probably just the American in me prattling on. But in some countries, history is incredibly important.

Kyoto, Japan, is a little like that. To me anyway. Kyoto is a city alive with history and tradition. Before Tokyo, Kyoto was the capital city of Japan. It's still considered by many Japanese to be the cultural center of the country. I mean *culture* as in history and tradition. In my opinion, culture is not something that can be attained by scheduling orchestral performances or art exhibits. Tokyo is massive and fashionable. Kyoto is rich and vibrant and it wears the history of Japan like a beautiful kimono.

The people of Kyoto are so in tune with their history and tradition, it influences even seemingly unrelated decisions. While there, I was told about a young man from Kyoto who was offered a position by a large company the day he graduated from college. He verbally accepted the position.

A few days later, another company offered him a better job, at a better salary, with more upward mobility.

After considering everything, the young man decided to go to work for the first company.

The reason he made that decision, to me as an American, is a little hard to relate to. His decision had almost nothing to do with the fact that he had verbally accepted the first position offered. He made the decision because the first company had historically sought out and hired students from the university he graduated from. He feared that if he didn't go to work there, the company might think poorly of his school and not hire future graduates.

Admirable? Yes, it is. I wish I could have met that young man.

Right or wrong, I possess no such depth of character and loyalty. If I hadn't signed a contract with the first company, my lips would've lost blood flow from the speed at which I got to the lobby of the second company.

Admirable? Not really.

As an American, I can't draw from the depth of historical context that most citizens of other countries can. It's not in me.

There is good and bad in that. My mind is not influenced by a four-thousand-year weight of societal influence and obligations, true. But there is something calming, something important, about a history like Japan's. America, by contrast, is less than 250 years old. No matter how admirable I find the reassuring effects of history and culture, my sample size is simply too limited.

But still, given my love of minutia, I've wondered, how many of my life choices are bogged down by historical elements that ought not to be considered? Where is the line between honoring the ancient paths of those who came before me and losing the path right in front of me? I started to think about all the random stuff I think about while thinking about specific stuff.

I'm easily distracted.

A Brief History of Whine

When working through issues of faith, the here and now is a much cleaner lens through which to view the providential hand of God.

At times, I've been consumed with the idea that I've inherited a "sin nature" from Adam, and it gets me all mentally twisty. I moan and cry about thistles, thorns, and stress. Inside I've lamented, "Why did they do it? Why did the fall in the garden of Eden have to be so complete? Why did one act of disobedience by people I never knew have to be so total in its devastation?"

When parents say, "Don't stand on that stool or you're going to get hurt," they don't truly think the action will result in anything more than a scraped knee or a bruised bum.

No parent ever says, "Don't run with those scissors or you and every other person who is ever born from this day forward will carry the head-to-toe disfiguring scars from your jogging indiscretion and will die."

But that's what happened with Adam and Eve.

Fully Mired in the Minutiae

Why am I so curious about stuff that doesn't benefit my walk or my witness? I've engaged in some really silly conversations and educational pursuits. I've debated what the actual fruit was Adam and Eve ate. I've pored over articles that painstakingly study historical documents to find out where the garden of Eden was likely located. I've been riveted while reading about a gaggle of historians estimating its size and borders.

Fascinating but relatively useless information sucks me in like pecan pie. Yummy.

I seldom seem to focus on the right questions. My gut tells me I should spend very little time caring about the sin nature I inherited or the exact location of the garden of Eden, but I should care immensely about what I lost in the garden and how I can get it back!

What I lost there is tragic. I lost my innocence.

I can't do anything, beyond what I did in accepting Jesus Christ, about that. What took place in the garden of Eden resulted in sin entering humankind, and now my body is fated to eventually become a worm farm. It happened. Yes, I still think about it from time to time.

But the sin itself is not the important part of what took place there.

I lost some seriously important stuff in the garden of Eden. I lost the perpetual peace of the Holy Spirit. What I lost there was the holiness of God being a part of my person. What I lost was the casual elegance of walking and talking with God in the cool of the evening. I lost absolutely everything of importance, and I want it back.

That's what should consume me. And you.

My sin nature should not drive me. What was removed from me should drive my every waking moment.

Verify and Then Move On

I'm not saying that detailed study is bad. If you want to settle in your mind the validity of Scripture based on the historical accuracy of Scripture, go for it. The descriptive history of the Bible is important to know and soak up.

But don't be paralyzed by the history when it comes to who you are today in Christ Jesus. It's part of our story only as far as it advances his glory. Beyond that, it's coffee-table-book information.

Did someone say coffee? Never mind, that was me.

The historical details might make us sound learned among friends, but not much more. The prescriptive elements of Scripture should merit a little more of our attention. That's where the real life-changing treasure is found.

There Are No Dumb Questions

Yes, there are.

If I went back to that baseball stadium, I would first look for my wallet in the lost and found department. I would ask the important questions and look in the right places. It's recoverable.

What I lost in the garden is no longer where I left it, though. It can now be claimed in a new lost and found department, on a hill between two thieves.

My garden of Eden God-wallet is still findable as long as I go to the right place, ask the important questions, and seek the right answers. (I can't prove it, but I bet that's the first time in history the previous line has ever been typed—and that thought pleases me greatly.)

Ask the real questions. Know what it is that you lost and how you can recover it.

The sacrifice of Jesus Christ was God's response to what we lost in the garden of Eden. The cool of the evening stroll is back and pretty close to the original. The gentle attending of the Holy Spirit is within earshot again.

These things can no longer be found in the garden of Eden, no matter how accurately we map it. No, you being naked and unashamed outdoors will never again be seen as appropriate, so let it go. Right now.

Japa-Knees

I love Kyoto. I love Japan—and its people. Japan is a remarkable country with a glorious and amazing past. It should be a source of comfort, confirmation, and pride for the people of Japan.

Our faith has a glorious and amazing past as well. But as Christians, what we draw from that past should end at comfort and confirmation.

Our faith offers no room for pride. Our past should drive us to our knees to honor the heritage we share. That's where it should end.

I think we all should be about the business of finding others, new faces in new places, that will respond to the call of God and join us on our knees.

.... *Shun Common* ....

Chapter: He's Taking Notes

Location: Seoul, South Korea

Purpose: Introductory Discussions

I've always enjoyed South Korea—specifically Seoul, the capital—but for the longest time I could never quite put a finger on why.

Seoul is a tough city. The culture seems to lack some of the refined honorifics you find in other Asian countries. And they fed me really odd food. At one particular meal, I recall being treated to some delicious barbequed cow intestines and acorn jelly.

Oh, just try to hold me back from getting seconds!

I kid.

I'm stunned my wife still kisses me. How it looked on my plate still haunts me. I needed eye bleach.

Needless to say, meals were not near the top of my to-do list in Seoul. And while there are some beautiful sights and incredible people in Seoul, it's still a sprawling, no-nonsense city. That's normally not my cup of kimchi.

But I would never hesitate to go back to Seoul. For some reason, even with all these quirks, like the city I did.

Vodka Burps

The guy I'm meeting in Seoul scowls, scratches, snorts, picks his teeth, and burps. A lot. He's wearing a wedding ring. I silently weep for HA! his wife. I'm in the lobby of a Hilton hotel with Jabba the Hutt.

Am I being pranked?

Nobody around us seems to notice or care. So I ride it through and wind up this anti-finishing-school experience. Afterward, to kill some time, I walk the streets around the hotel. I feel at home there.

I end up having dinner at the hotel restaurant. I'm not much of a drinker, but when eating alone, the bar always feels like a reasonable place to land. I feel silly sitting at a table for four by myself.

I'm drinking iced tea and the guy next to me is consuming vodka tonics like potatoes and distillation are being outlawed in the morning.

Thirty minutes later, his arm is on my shoulder and he's crying. Interesting.

He is lamenting the hostilities that once existed between our countries and desperately hoping he and I can become friends. I decide not to let him know that I'm leaving in the morning just in case that news compels him to accelerate the friendship process.

It was a, um, magical evening.

Still, in spite of a few odd experiences, I have more than pleasant memories and feelings about Korea and its people. It wasn't until sometime later that I heard something that explained why I was so fond of the country.

I read an article about languages and learned that the Korean language contains an unusual mix of pitch and tonal qualities. That was it!

I've always liked the sound of pitch languages. A pitch language uses a rise or fall in voice inflection to differentiate words and meaning, like Japanese and Swedish. Stress languages like English and Arabic, on the other hand, use volume and emphasis to indicate key words in a sentence. Stress languages feel tense by design to me.

But the Korean language incorporates elements of tone and pitch. It was soothing and melodic and set me at ease. Even if I didn't understand a single word of it.

But how could something as pedestrian as tone and pitch cause me to overlook any other less than festive experiences I had in Korea?

The answer was simpler than I'd imagined. I love music. All kinds of music. I felt like all of Seoul was singing to me.

But why was its influence so powerful on me?

I finally arrived at the answer, but the path wasn't so direct. So, I'll get to my point by an equally circuitous route. Fun for you. Fun for me.

Do You Hear Yourself?

How long did you believe in the Santa scam when you were a child?

I don't recall my age when I was told, or discovered, it was all a ruse. I don't even recall being particularly disappointed. I was ambivalent. But at some point, my ambivalence turned to embarrassment that I had ever believed a salad bar–avoiding chap in a sleigh could deliver gifts to every child in the world in one night.

I used to have that same feeling of gullibility when I told people that God sees every action and hears every word of every person on the planet. No matter how many times I ran it around inside my noggin, I just couldn't quite stomp the juice out of this theological grape.

Maybe it seemed even more unbelievable to me because I wasn't sure why God would even want to hear the incessant yammering of a rebellious world. The constant din of the dim would be exhausting to me. Nevertheless, I still wanted to find some way to think about this all-seeing, omnipresent truth so the visions of this sugarplum-shaped conundrum would stop dancing in my head—or at least not in *Riverdance* mode.

Thank You, Ernst

Then I learned of an eighteenth-century German scientist and musician named Ernst Chladni. Because of his love of science and music, he became a pioneer in the science of sound and acoustics.

In his most famous experiment, Chladni showed how moving a violin bow against a metal plate covered in fine sand would show the movement of the sound. More than just moving the sand, though, he discovered that notes and frequencies contain patterns. If you produced the same note at the same frequency on the metal plate, the sand would form the same unique pattern.

Notes have shape. Who knew?

If you've never seen this, you need to. The device is called a Chladni plate and the science is called cymatics.

YouTube it. Go on. I'll still be here when you get back.

A Little Sap

Warning: this theory is out-there, even for me. I'm only telling you how I was able to come to spiritual grips with something as unfathomable as an omnipresent God.

It's what I do. I hope it helps you as well.

I'm going to propose something a little sappy and a great deal trite, which I am usually loathe to do. But this particular font farm of smarm actually helped me sneak a peek at a snippet of God's being that had previously eluded me. I hope my man cave won't be repossessed because of this admission. If I can actually explain it to you, this might even be a redeemable chapter!

Let's think about notes and symbols in a different way.

Imagine our lives are an epic novel, or a timeless song, that is uniquely ours. God has a glorious story of redemption and conquest to tell, and it is up to us to fill the pages. Imagine that from the foundations of the earth, God composed a song that is mine or yours alone. Imagine that the notes of our song are struck by our individual acts of Christlike service.

Maybe our obedience reaches God's ears as a pleasing melody. Maybe our own personal song is, quite literally, music to his ears. Take me, for instance. Maybe he doesn't hear my words as much as he hears the purity of my notes and the beauty of my song. Maybe my prayers sound like a love song of relationship. Maybe that's what God hears. Maybe the flat or sharp notes of our disobedience cause his head to tilt and his ear to incline toward the offending minstrel. Most likely me.

I'm no musician and my voice is average at best. I'm not a good judge of vocal talent. But when someone is flat or sharp, even when they are singing with others, my ears immediately pick it up. I don't hear individual harmonies and voices when they are on pitch—I just hear the music. But an off note sticks out to me like a maraschino cherry–sized pimple on the forehead of the prom queen. Maybe that's how God keeps tabs on this whole creation cacophony.

God gave us music. It stands to reason that he would use it for his glory. Music is powerful. It draws us, moves us, and binds us. So much so for me that it redefined how I thought about an entire country. They fed me barbequed cow intestines! And I still like Korea.

That's some powerful melodic voodoo.

In the same way and by the blood of Jesus, God forgives my off notes because he loves to hear my life sing to him. Off pitch and all, God longs to hear all of our songs.

I don't know for sure, but I like to believe that music is somehow deeper and more significant to God than any of us knows.

Sounds or Shapes?

Since we now know notes and frequencies have shapes, maybe as our life song is performed it is simultaneously recorded as shapes—just like on the Chladni plates.

Maybe these shapes, these holy hieroglyphs, tell an epic tale of redemption, relationship, and love. Words, sentences, paragraphs, and chapters perfectly transcribed so there's never any question as to who the author and finisher of our faith truly is. Maybe these characters form the Rosetta Stone of our faith, unlocking the intimate and secret language of God the Father. Maybe more than our names are recorded in the Lamb's book of life.

Hey, it's not called the Lamb's ledger of life. You with me?

I wonder what the notes and shapes of grace and mercy sound and look like. Sacrificial love has to be a note that pierces the dark and rings clearly above all the other noise of an unrepentant world. If God looks down and sees the unique symbols that my life song should form and hears the perfectly composed notes of my individual song, maybe he just closes his eyes and enjoys the concert.

Maybe?

Shun Common

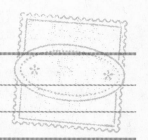

Chapter: God Did What?

Location: Larnaca, Cyprus

Purpose: Expansion Discussions

Turkey is a decidedly Islamic country with a secular government. Sitting roughly fifty miles off its coast in the Mediterranean Sea is the island country of Cyprus.

Stay with me. There's a point to my brief geography lesson.

The relationship between Cyprus and Turkey is so bad that you can't fly directly to it from Turkey, only fifty miles away. To get here I had to fly to Athens, Greece, and get a connecting flight.

It was worth it. Cyprus is almost entirely Greek Orthodox and stunningly beautiful. Many of the cafés and restaurants have outdoor-only seating with vined trellises providing filtered shade. The streets are bright and full of life and the architecture is both ancient and colorful. I loved it.

I was in the city of Larnaca, where the people were warm and thoroughly unashamed of their Greek heritage. Some of you might be thinking about a particular movie right now. I am too. If not, I'll give you a few paragraphs to figure out which film.

I was there to discuss the potential of opening coffee shops in this enjoyable island country. I was set to meet with the current CEO of the company, who was the grandchild of the company founder. The company was looking to branch out from its import and export roots, and I was there to see if it made sense for my company to be a part of that process.

I arrived late enough in the day that they took me straight to my waterfront hotel. Liked that idea. After some introductory banter in the lobby, we decided to meet in the morning. No meeting till morning?

Excellent! Since my room was quite nice and had a balcony that looked
out onto the Mediterranean Sea, I was all in on that plan.

The next morning they took me directly to the company headquar-
ters. I joined the CEO of the company in his large but understated office.
Conversation was pleasant, comfortable, and productive. After the introductory pleasantries he raised his hand to put our conversation on hold
and ask if I'd like coffee.

The blood content in my caffeine stream was a little high so I quickly
nodded my approval.

He went to the door, opened it, and gave an unseen individual some
quick instructions. He returned to his chair and the conversation
recommenced until the door opened again and a young man entered
with a tray. On the tray were traditional coffee implements from this
part of the world. As he prepared our drinks, he issued a warning.

They always do to Americans.

He told me their coffee was much stronger and contained much more
sediment than I was accustomed to. I'd had this type of coffee in many
countries, but I was amused by the warning and stayed silent.

After my first sip, I smiled my approval and commented, "It's prepared in the Turkish style."

Without a moment's hesitation or any sign of uncertainty, this came
out of his mouth: "Yes, some people call it Turkish style, but it was orig- ohoh
inally Greek!"

I couldn't stop from laughing out loud. My bad.

I seldom laugh out loud, especially in a business setting. He didn't,
but some of you know why I laughed. I had inadvertently found my way
onto the real-life set of *My Big Fat Greek Wedding*. The way he uttered the
phrase was exactly the way it was stated in the movie. I quickly scanned
his bookshelves for Windex. The moment was priceless and still makes
me smile, inside and out. I'm writing this chapter in a coffee shop and
smiling like a half-wit right now.

Ah, let 'em wonder.

I'd been in the coffee industry for a long time and knew full well that
it really was a Turkish-style coffee preparation. But I let my Greek friend

own it that day. The moment was too perfect to spoil it with silly ole reality.

Credit or Blame

Aside from being amazing, the experience made me wonder how often I take credit for something that really isn't my own and, more importantly, how often I give God credit for something that isn't entirely his.

Imagine this scene. You and a couple of friends are sitting one evening in a Christian coffee shop. The conversation is animated and the coffee delicious. You notice a musician in the corner setting up to perform. Ten minutes later, the lights dim and the same semi-disheveled fellow mounts a stool and adjusts his microphone. Rather than play, he clears his throat.

You know what's coming and you preemptively fire up your auto-cringe unit.

Then he says it: "I'm going to play a song for you that God gave me."

How Nice of God

I know what you're thinking. *Did he really give you that? God? Wow! You two must be tight.* Or, maybe you're screaming inside, *Please be great!*

Then he strums the most disjointed of chord changes possible on his guitar, and even though his voice is reasonable, the song is no tasty dish of musical composition. To be sure, your dog would be challenged to choke it down.

When I hear the "God claim" in musical circles, my conclusion is as certain as my mauled expectations. I'm either completely incapable of recognizing musical perfection and the holy notes were somehow lost in the celestial translation, or God truly sucketh at songwriting.

Or I Must Have Missed It

I've read the Bible—a lot. I just don't recall the specific passage where Jesus admonishes us to blame our mediocre mud on him.

Why is it that once we become a Christian, we feel it's our solemn duty to blame God for almost everything—even when the actions don't merit the association? Do we think it exonerates us from responsibility for the work? Is it supposed to look better if we distance ourselves from the result? Do we do it to stifle any genuine critique of the finished product?

Why isn't it okay to say something like, "Well, I'm fairly new to songwriting and I realize it may be rough, but here's a tune I wrote to honor my Savior"?

Hear me here. Musicians, play on. Singers, belt it out. Writers, set pen to paper. Artists, slather that oil.

But be cautious about whose noggin you're blowing that origin spitball at.

Verily, Verily (I Love the Phrase)

Let's square up here.

There's a difference between acknowledging God's hand of influence and lordship in our lives and boasting of God's sovereign, miraculous authorship of any given action or work. The distinction is subtle but may determine how others perceive God through us. I think we should take very seriously our representation of what God is capable of in us.

If the times I publicly nod to God are less than stellar, what have I actually done for the perception of God Almighty in others? I sing about his glory and greatness in church on Sunday and mock him with my mediocrity the rest of the week.

This can't be a good thing.

Claim Jumping

As a youth, my life was chock-full of deception, laziness, irresponsibility, and selfishness. Yep, as I have said before, I was quite a catch! Marrying over my head and scrambling to be a good husband played a significant role in my reclamation. I would say God performed miracles. *cute* The world would say I finally grew up.

The world points to its own standard of progress. People usually get better at handling and saving money as they get older. Many become more skilled and trusted in their profession as they age. As people age and gain life experience, their emotional maturity often follows suit. These things are not exclusive to Christians.

But shouldn't we be different?

If the only things I attribute to God are things that keep pace with the world's standards, what am I actually boasting about? I have unsaved friends who, in their youth, were just as pathetic as I was. Today, many of them are fantastic fathers, dependable workers, loyal spouses, and honest friends to those around them.

Me-diocrity

Only attributing the remarkable to God doesn't mean we stop doing anything.

Take my writing for example. I could simply wait until such a time as I believed the words here to be one-hundred-percent scripted by God (not going to happen), or I can use the mind and desire that God gave me and exercise my albeit limited but current level of ability. The only way I will get better at this writing thing is to subject people like you to the process.

By the way, I really appreciate it.

As my ability to recite the words of the Father increases, so then should the wisdom and maturity with which I convey them.

Will I attribute all that is sound in this book to Christ Jesus? Absolutely!

Will I boast of the direct authorship of God in these pages? Not on your life!

In doing so, I would be placing my writing on the same level as Scripture, and that's not a vacation spot I care to visit. God is capable of so much more through me than what I can exhibit at this time.

But that will never, and should never, prevent me from operating on God's behalf with all my effort. I truly believe that if I'm walking in faith and doing things for the right reasons, God can accomplish the miraculous, in spite of my less than perfect results.

What's the Big Deal?

My Cypriot friend claiming a false origin for the Turkish coffee preparation technique didn't make the java taste any better. Or worse. It humored me and still does.

But within that humor lurked a subtle undercurrent of suspicion. Even with the current hostilities between Cyprus and Turkey, why did he need to claim an origin that wasn't accurate? I found myself questioning other claims he made, even when the statements were verifiably true. Maybe he actually believed it to be true. But that wouldn't settle my doubt either.

How is that different from the things I push off on God when the results of the action scream otherwise? How much of what we portray about our lives involves some level of revisionist history? Are there anecdotes in this book that have been embellished over the years for the sake of impact?

Okay, my feet are getting a little toasty. Next question! (I'm kidding. Lord, I hope not!)

With my Cypriot friend's claim, I didn't question the people of Turkey; I questioned the credibility of my friend. It was a wake-up call for me. The unintended consequences of my own bravado, no matter how well intentioned, can chip away at how others see me and, by association, my Savior.

And I won't go there.

The longer I live, the more conscious I am of God's reputation as seen through my actions and words. No, God does not need me to prop up his reputation. His standing and authority are just fine on their own.

I just don't want to be that guy. That guy who reduces anyone's perception of the Lord of glory by haphazardly pinning his actions and words on God.

Give God honor, praise, and glory, not blame.

·············· Shun Common ···

Chapter: Witness for the Persecution

Location: All over the World

Purpose: Listening to Drunk People

My father-in-law, one of the wisest men I know, once told me, "If you really want to know what a man thinks, get him drunk or knock him down."

There's truth to this axiom. I've met thousands of people from all over the world in my twenty-five-plus-year career in the international coffee industry. The vast majority were genuinely pleasant people. There were some, though.

Wow, were there some . . .

On these occasions, it definitely wasn't the coffee talking. In many countries, alcohol is a social balm applied liberally in the evening hours. Once adequately slathered, tongues often get quite loose.

Personal slights, ethnic shots, anti-American comments, and jabs at my faith. This type of stuff honestly never bothers me. I don't know why, but as long as my Lord and my family love me, I don't need much more fondness directed at me. Again, comments like these were extremely rare, but they did happen. As long as my personal safety was not at risk, I met these comments with a calm smile and a casual nod.

You might be thinking to yourself that I exhibited an admirable amount of godly self-control in these situations.

Nope.

I just didn't care that much. And I knew they would like me again once they sobered up. No harm, no foul. Laceration-free evenings are the best!

And most importantly, I'm always conscious of what I call what. Terms are important to me. Very.

Race Is Not Part of My Spiritual Race

I'm going to make a comparison that might make some of you feel uncomfortable because of the history and politics associated with it. Nevertheless, I believe the comparison to be sound.

I believe overt racism is one of the most insidious and ungodly thought processes anyone can give themselves over to. Few things shame me about my country like the institution of slavery that once poisoned the humanity-well of this land. It's one of the most pervasive evils ever engaged in by otherwise God-fearing men and women.

Because of my disgust for racism and bigotry, I am equally repulsed when someone claims racism or bigotry when the actual circumstance does not merit the assertion. If you're a genuinely rotten employee and you get sacked, it's not racism or bigotry. Own it. Calling it anything else is irresponsible and harmful. When any accusation is made and used to gain advantage, intimidate, or game the system, those witnessing the event could slowly become desensitized to actual, honest instances of real, soulless racism and bigotry.

I don't know what's worse, wearing down people's outrage against racism and bigotry with false claims of it or the legitimate instance itself. Both activities destroy people, but false claims of racism and bigotry slowly liquefy the bedrock of authenticity and disfigure the God-breathed beauty of the ideal.

Chowderheads and Nicks

The same standard holds true for Christians when it comes to what we call persecution.

The Bible tells me that, as a Christian, I'll be persecuted for the sake of righteousness. It tells me the testing fire of adversity is part and parcel with being a follower of Jesus Christ. The instruction to pick up my cross and follow Jesus is a sobering responsibility and not a milquetoast undertaking.

But I need to be careful.

The Internet is loaded with instances of horrific acts of violence around the world against believers for simply proclaiming Jesus as Lord. But all persecution is not equal.

Being verbally assaulted for your faith is not always a sign of your righteousness. In my Christian life the presence of slander was sometimes nothing more than a sign that I was behaving like a weirdo. Other times it was just a tiny nick to my pride from an uninformed or inebriated source. Big deal.

I've seen American Christians actively behave in a way that seeks out verbal reprisals solely so they can bask in the counterfeit glow of an unlikeable righteousness. I've been present in restaurants when Christians have left Bible verses scrawled on a napkin instead of leaving a tip. Sad. But wait, there's more! Then they had the temerity to tell their server what they did and say it was the most valuable thing they could leave them. How embarrassing. They sought out the response from the server in their final miserly act. They were broke, cheap, or mean, not righteous.

 I secretly hoped they went back to that same restaurant days later and got to enjoy a nice saliva burger, compliments of the kitchen staff. I'm a bad man.

Sincerely following Jesus in the United States is seldom met with actual persecution. To be sure, some form of persecution-lite will find me as surely as a chubby kid will spot a doughnut shop. That's a given.

But for the sake of my witness and my international brothers and sisters in Christ, I need to go easy on the terminology.

Not All Harm Is Immediate

You might be asking, "What's the big deal?" Persecution is persecution. If someone is mean enough to persecute you just because you're acting like a chowderhead, they are clearly mean enough to persecute you just because you're a Christian as well. A bully is a bully is a bully, right?

Ye-es, it's true that many who demean others do so because they are simply mean, mad, insecure, or stupid. But that's not the real issue or the real danger here.

Crying "wolf" on persecution is harmful for the same reason unjustifiably crying racism is. It erodes the contrast. Even more, it dishonors the sacrifice of others around the world who live in constant terror of government reprisals or violence at the hands of another worldview.

When we water down the meaning of the word *persecution*, we weaken the resolve of nonbelievers to be outraged by it.

If your personality is a little wonky, that's okay. Buck up and own it. Don't blame it on persecution. As I've said, my personality is a bit of a tire fire. I'm a target-rich environment for anyone who cares to mock. It comes with the territory of Ron.

But that's where it needs to end. People around the world are being tortured and executed for proclaiming Jesus as Lord, so I have no business grousing about verbal mosquito bites. As Americans, we have almost no idea what real persecution is. We may understand the concept of persecution, but we in this country have almost no clue as to what constitutes real-life persecution beyond our shores.

If your family no longer talks to you because you accepted Jesus as Lord, you're being snubbed or, at worst, ostracized. If you are being made to fear for your physical safety because you serve Jesus Christ, you're being persecuted.

If people make fun of you and think your Christian beliefs are a silly crutch, you're being criticized. If you're routinely dragged from your bed and beaten in the middle of the night, you're being persecuted.

If you've been passed over for a promotion or not hired because you follow Jesus, you're being discriminated against. If you've ever spent an extended period of time in prison solely because you proclaim Jesus as Lord, you're being persecuted.

It's important we understand the difference between experiencing obstacles and prejudice and living under true persecution.

Cotton Candy Candid

Perspective is an amazing thing.

If we actually knew firsthand what was happening to Christians around the world for simply being Christians, we would be hard-pressed to ever legitimately proclaim persecution here. It makes even the notion of suggesting persecution for the silly verbal inconveniences we experience seem like accusation cotton candy. It looks all puffed up and tasty. But the second you ask the rest of the world to swallow it, it reveals itself as the spun sugar and air that it is.

The people who despised Jesus were the religious elite and the power brokers of the age. But the saved and unsaved desperately wanted to be around Jesus. They clamored to hear him. They would brave crowds and risk personal injury just to touch the hem of his garment. They fervently sought his notice, even if it meant being lowered to him from a rooftop.

Do ordinary people, saved and unsaved, want to be around us?

Be honest. It's an important thing for us to know about ourselves. God can't fix what we won't confess.

My Confession to You

Some may take issue with my book, or portions of it. I might get a few five-star reviews; I'm almost certain to get one-star reviews.

Is that kind of criticism "persecution"?

Not even close. My intention is good. My skin is thick (I hope). I'll let the rest of the public-opinion leaves fall and settle on the soil of my heart. At the end of the day, they'll help me grow. Thank you very mulch.

But I shouldn't stop there. I need to carry that resilience into the rest of my walk with Christ. I need to honor those around the world who live every day with real persecution by never, ever using the term haphazardly or as a means to condone my being daft. For this guy, there is simply too great a risk for too many people to justify the proportionately safe saints of the world to ever feign peril or marginalize martyrdom.

I might never experience the level of persecution that Christians in other parts of the world do. But I can guard my tongue and their sacrifice by letting the appropriate titles belong to the ones who have earned it with their very blood.

············· Shun Common ·············

Chapter: An Affinity for Salinity

Location: Dubai, United Arab Emirates

Purpose: Contract Negotiation

There's lots of money in Dubai.

Understatement. When I say lots of money, I mean copious bucka-roos. It's awash in money. The country itself is a sandy poster child for affluence and irrigation.

The world's most expensive cars are everywhere on the streets. If you so choose, you can stay in hotel rooms that have solid gold fixtures. Incredible yachts are everywhere in the marinas. The highest fashion, the best food, and the most elaborate nightlife are all on display in Dubai. The man-made beauty here is eye-popping. The world's dependence on oil has transformed this otherwise barren wasteland into a flourishing Mecca of business, vacations, and excess. The opulence of Dubai rivals anything one might see anywhere in the world.

So from that standpoint, it's easy to feel relatively safe there. Unlike other parts of the Middle East, in Dubai I can comfortably be the salt Jesus called me to be, seasoning the world around me. It's not as well received by the locals as it would be in Nebraska, but hey, it's not forbidden either.

Visa Unease

Doing business here has taken away—for now anyway—a few bucket-list destinations for me.

Surprisingly the greatest risk for me here would be a visa stamp in my passport from Israel. If I were to travel to Israel for any reason and then travel to Dubai or any other Middle Eastern country, the level of suspicion and contempt from every customs authority would be ratcheted up tenfold. I could be detained, searched, harassed, and denied future entry into their country.

This has always been a disappointing reality for me. So today, you and I are going to pretend. We're going to wipe the travel slate clean and imagine that the world is wide open to us. If there were no concern for safety, where in the world would you want to go?

Actually, since this is my book and I make the rules, let's narrow the question to a Bible destination.

No whining. It was in the small print. Never mind—it's all in small print.

If you could visit any place in the Bible, where would it be?

I'll go first. My choice? The Dead Sea. With that name? Has to be at the top of my to-visit list. In my early twenties I figured they called it the Dead Sea because a disproportionate number of people drowned there every year. Or maybe it was the fashionable place to scatter the ashes of the deceased. I do love a good pyre cremation ceremony.

The true reason it's called the Dead Sea is, of course, a bit more mundane. The Dead Sea is too salty for almost anything to live in it. No fish, no kelp, no coral, no nothing. It's seven times saltier than the Atlantic or Pacific Ocean. The concentration is so great that salt just piles up in mounds on the floor of the Dead Sea.

We all need salt to live, but as the Dead Sea proves, in sufficient concentrations it becomes a deadly substance that can kill any living creature—even Elvis impersonators.

Salt Minds

In proper amounts, salt can take a food from good to scrumptious.

In Matthew 5, in the Sermon on the Mount, God tells me to be the salt of the earth. He follows up that directive with a question: "But if the salt [me again] loses its saltiness, how can it be made salty again?" He tells me my role and then asks what will happen if I don't fulfill that role. It's not a question if I *can* make the world more delicious but if I *will*.

This Christianity stuff is so much work.

Unfortunately, in following Jesus, too often I seem to gravitate toward the confines of the saltshaker. I like church. Often it feels more spiritual to hang out only with those who call themselves followers of Christ. Sometimes I justify this by being on the front lines in other areas of the world.

However, I've learned that any Christian-only association in my social world can result in a Dead Sea environment. My brothers and sisters in Christ are salt as well. My salt self, along with the other grains, no longer has a seasoning quality but becomes concentrated to the point of making the environment uninhabitable to outsiders.

I'm More Stable on My Toes

My spiritual isolationism can foster insider information that nobody else but other Christians can decipher, further isolating me from the people I claim to want to reach.

When I come home from other countries, melting back into my Christianity camp feels justified. I can let my guard down and rest. Christianity has a big network. I mean, we have our own music. We have our own movies. We have our own books. We have our own politics, jokes, icons, events, and churchspeak. But developing forms of church insider communication that the unsaved can't understand can lead to our criticism of anyone beyond the walls of our exclusive little clubs.

I can't get complacent. I need to be back on my toes, mixing it up with the lost. I can feel the need pulling at me. It's how I'm built. It's what I was made to do.

This salt-only type of existence, even for a season, can't possibly be what God had in mind for my life when he gave the Great Commission. The Great Commission, *my* Great Commission, can only be engaged when I'm living alongside, in relationship with, and serving those who don't yet know Jesus. Then and only then will my salty character be of eternal, kingdom-expanding value.

If I just wanted to belong to a club, I should have joined PETA, the Elks, or the Shriners. No costly meat, considerably more liquor, lots of silly hats.

The lure of a silly hat can be strong.

I'm comfortable around other Christians. But I can't allow myself to live in an environment so salty that it becomes toxic to any nonbeliever unfortunate enough to stray into its social waters.

Salt Statues Suck

Consider Lot's wife. Because of her rearview rebellion, God turned her into a big ole chunk of salt. She became a pillar of the community, but not the kind that is envied. Her entire existence was reduced to a substance that would deteriorate, crumble, and be absorbed by the earth—leaving no sign of her existence. Her Morton moment seems to me to make a rather clear statement about the utter ineffectiveness of a salt-only existence.

I was meant to season my communities, not saturate small, exclusive enclaves of them that are already salty themselves. I cannot season a seasoning with more of the seasoning itself.

Insulating myself from the harsh glare of a different worldview might be easy, comfortable, and even fun, but it is not what I was created for.

A Low Point

Did you know that the shoreline of the Dead Sea is the lowest point of dry land on the planet? The shores of the Dead Sea measure at a mind-numbing 1,291 feet below sea level. That's foghorn low, people!

While a salt-saturated life might not be blatantly indifferent toward the unsaved, it may well be, like the shores of the Dead Sea, the lowest possible point of expression in our call to reach the lost for Jesus.

The spiritual battle is always raging. I can't continue to chase the mirage of the church-immersion oasis. It's not really there.

Take a chance with me. Step out beyond our salty circles and do a little mingling in the land of bland. Let's elevate our God-game and spend some time on the terra firma T-bone.

Scary? Sometimes it is. But I think we'll both be amazed at how much we have to offer. We're called to the front lines to flavor the world. Even when being on the front lines keeps us from fulfilling other things on our personal wish list. I'll be there when the time is right, Israel. It's a small price to pay. Until then, I'll pray for you and look forward to it. There will come a time.

Remember: tasty saint? Delicious! Toxic clique? Not so good.

·············· — *Shun Common* ··

Chapter: I'm Just Ducky

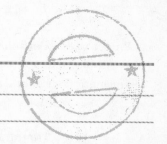

Location: Me

Purpose: To Do Something

I'm going to end this book by poking a little fun at myself. Truth is, I like few things as much as laughing at myself and being transparent about my flaws if it encourages and builds the body of Christ. For whatever reason, it soaks my cereal.

So let's dive in to my warts and all, but first a quick setup: I've never been bothered by the fact that Christianity is a tough faith to walk out. (Isn't that the point?) Truth is, if not for grace and mercy, I'd have tossed out my salvation lottery ticket a long time ago. Wouldn't even have checked the numbers . . . or Deuteronomy. I'm pretty sure my clinging need for mercy is the spiritual stall I'm supposed to park my faith in. I like being here.

So this chapter—and for that matter, this book—isn't for those who misguidedly imagine they have it all together in Jesus. If you were voted most likely to succeed in school and you believed it, this probably isn't your bowl of bisque either. It's not for those lamenting a facet of their physical makeup. Your feet look just fine.

This one's for the oddballs. The flawed like me. (If you've made it this far in my book, you're probably a little off-kilter yourself.)

It's a shout-out to the expats from the Island of Misfit Boys and Girls. It's a snoot-filling snort of smelling salts for those people whose lives, knowingly or unknowingly, perpetually brew up a piping hot mug of weirdo-joe.

My Malady

You've heard the phrase, "He (or she) is an odd duck." If you're a worship team member or a youth pastor, you've heard it often.

Thanks for the kinship by the by.

In my youth, I always felt like an odd duck. Not your garden-variety, run-of-the-mill odd duck, mind you. I'm talking a steroid-enhanced, weapons-grade, antibiotic-resistant strain of waddle-oozing oddness. My personality seemed as socially dependable as a narcoleptic chaperone at senior prom.

Even today I have this gnawing suspicion that some internal status quo cog was stripped of its teeth in my early development and now just spins freely inside me, the machine.

When everyone else sees a spiritual issue as a bright, shiny red ball, I always see it as dull, oblong, and some shade of puce. To me it still looks like a ball, but not one that's capable of a predictable bounce.

I barely graduated high school. I was pitiful at academics. I didn't officially flunk birth but I did most everything else. I don't possess any certifications or credentials of any kind except being a child of the one true King.

I just try things. Business ventures that outkick my financial coverage? Yep. I give 'em a run. I try things without asking myself the question, "Am I qualified?" I already know the answer. I built and sold a company for more money than I could have ever imagined. God has been extravagant and gracious with me. I have also gone bankrupt. So, yes, I know the highs, but I'm also intimately familiar with the place underneath the bottom of the barrel.

Because of these things, I fall down a lot in my Christian walk. I feel like I'm stuck in a vertical-horizontal, rinse-and-repeat rut. If I were going slowly, the repeated falls wouldn't seem so traumatic. Unfortunately, I'm usually heading down the path at a clip that would make most astronauts dry heave. Nobody else seems to have the same skin-to-scab ratio as I do. Staying down for a while would seem reasonable. Getting up quickly seems like it does nothing more than increase the frequency of my disfiguring crashes, but rise and bolt I do.

Good times, pleasant thoughts! I should write greeting cards.

I think about and say some odd things. During a trip to the Midwest with my wife, we went to see a few Amish communities. Everyone else

was admiring their beautiful farms and the uncluttered simplicity
of their lives. I only wanted to know if an Amish child was called an
"omelet."

I once requested that the fresh perch and prime rib dinner combo
I had ordered be divided into two plates. I told the waitress this was
necessary because I felt very strongly about the separation of "perch and
steak." The waitress just stared at me. My social appropriateness was so
faint that she could only trust in its existence due to my exhibition of
basic motor skills.

I sort my M&M's by color and eat them in a specific order. I bounce
a little when I walk even when I'm not happy. I don't like book covers.
Touching velvet gives me goose bumps and the spongy consistency of
mushrooms feels like sautéed eraser in my mouth—they taste okay,
though. I don't repair cars or do plumbing, and a utopian existence to
me is a place where Jane Austen was never born.

Coming Clean

Okay, truth be told, I'm not as completely disillusioned about who
I am as I might have indicated up to this point. And no, it wasn't self-
esteem classes or positive-affirmation workshops that turned me
around.

It was more direct than that. It was the realization that the things
that make me odd also make me uniquely crafted to serve and glorify
God in a way that only I was designed for. There are people who need to
hear what I have inside me. My journey was and is for a reason. It has
a purpose beyond getting me to this stage of life. If not used for God's
glory, it is nothing but squandered breaths and heartbeats. No matter
how pedestrian and uneventful, or self-destructive and tragic, it's all
suitable for ministry.

Deal with it.

You and I are masterfully crafted and painstakingly thought out.
God considered our every feature and idiosyncrasy when forming us.
He is so well pleased by us that he is willing to sign his name on us, his
masterpieces, using the blood of his Son.

The Clock Is Ticking

There is no better time than now for you to grasp this. Shockingly, there is no more qualified candidate to do God's work than you. We need to get comfortable with our all and our call.

You're odd. So what?

The world's definition of normal is a myth. It's an embarrassingly weak little bog fog that dissipates with even the slightest light of understanding directed at it. It's a fabrication fostered by the same type of arrogance that could not recognize the Christ, even when he walked among us.

God intended to make you as you are.

I'm talking about your personality and your quirks—not your sin. Don't try to pretend that your sin is somehow a unique personality characteristic or you will warp the beauty of this truth. Using our sin as an identity results in a spiritual life that emits lots of heat but very little light.

Let your understanding of this be simple and clean. God intended to make you as you are. Exactly as you are. Exactly. Let that understanding make you smile. I mean really smile. The kind of smile that if you had a dollop of whipped cream on your lips your ears would end up with some on them as well.

Oddly Godly

Let your insecurities die and then bury them. Don't embalm them and prop them up in the corner to point at when spiritual resignation or self-doubt feels like the easiest way forward.

You might be saying to yourself, *I already know this stuff.* Maybe you do. *There's nothing new here!* You would be right about that. But if most Christians truly grasped how intentionally they were crafted, they would live their lives differently and the church would not be as timid and ineffective as it is today.

God creates the fascinatingly unique. You are you and "you" is a good thing. You get me?

Without Jesus, I'm no great slice of pizza. I'm just a guy. I'm just a guy who is willing to try stuff. If I can write a book and get a person like you to read it, you can do almost anything.

I hope my book made you think, laugh a little, and shrug off the unreasonable limitations imposed by others—or yourself.

Common is easy. Shun it! We were not created to wallow in the mundane!

A duck's quack may not echo, but an odd duck's quack can move mountains.

Misfit? No. Beautifully unique? Without question. Embrace it!

We have kingdom work to do. Quack on, my friend.

Shun Common

Acknowledgments

I would like to express my gratitude—but decided against it. *Gratitude* is such a formal, stuffy-sounding word.

I would like to primal-scream my fist-pumping thanks to the men and women in my life who gave me just enough encouragement to annoy me and just enough good-natured ribbing to challenge me during the writing of this book.

James L. Rubart, you're a totally heinous friend. (And I mean that in the very best way possible.) You're an unbelievable inspiration to me and a reasonable golfer to many. Special shout-outs to John C. Stoller; Lori Roeleveld; Gary Shaffer; Don Daoust; Kregel Publications; my wife, Tina; daughter, Danielle; son, Riley; and anyone else who dismissively punched me in the arm and told me to get it done—you people are the coolest cats I know.

I'm eternally thankful for all of you . . . unless of course this book bombs. If that happens, then, with the obvious exception of my family, you're all dead to me. This is your fault.

I kid! Nothin' but love for all you infidels. I count myself blessed to have every single one of you in the corner I routinely paint myself into. It's kind of cozy.

The field awaits. Let's plow.

Ron DeMiglio

About the Author

Ron DeMiglio is a lifelong serial entrepreneur, speaker, and tireless advocate for the off-kilter Christians among us. He was one of only three businesspeople in the United States asked to speak in Washington, DC, about sustainable business models and corporate ethics before 250 international trade delegates. Ron sold his last coffee-related company in the fall of 2015 and, at that time, decided to give this whole writing thing a shot. You just read the result of that decision. The success, or failure, of this book will largely determine his next endeavor. No pressure, though. He doesn't like tofu, shag carpet, olives, or smooth jazz. Just so you know. Ron has lived in Washington State his entire life and is the forever husband of the most remarkable woman on earth. Together, and against the advice of casual observers everywhere, they reproduced and had a daughter, Danielle, and a son, Riley, both of whom are the best people Ron has ever known.